CANADIAN *Culinary* ROAD TRIP

Potato farm on Prince Edward Island

CANADIAN
Culinary
ROAD TRIP

TORMONT

Text: Isabel Fonte and Nathalie Vallière
Culinary consultants: Georges Chauvet and Gerry Philippe
Original idea: Gourmextra Inc.
Graphic design: Lorna Mulligan
Translation of recipes: Line Plante and Katrin Sermat
Recipe photos: Tango Photographie
© Tormont Publications Inc. for photographs of recipes and accessories
  as well as maps and itineraries.

TORMONT

© 2004 Tormont Publications Inc.
338 Saint Antoine Street East
Montreal, Canada H2Y 1A3
Tel. (514) 954-1441
Fax (514) 954-5086
www.tormont.com

Canadä
The publisher thanks Heritage Canada for the support awarded
under the Book Publishing Industry Development Program.

Legal deposit—Bibliothèque nationale du Québec, 2004

Printed in China

French River, PEI

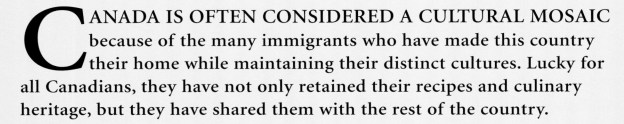

CANADA IS OFTEN CONSIDERED A CULTURAL MOSAIC because of the many immigrants who have made this country their home while maintaining their distinct cultures. Lucky for all Canadians, they have not only retained their recipes and culinary heritage, but they have shared them with the rest of the country.

Some of these culinary imports are new, having arrived in the past few decades from Asia, South America and Africa. Others arrived with early European settlers over the past few hundred years and, in some regions, have become part of the traditional Canadian culinary landscape.

In large cities, you can savour food from the four corners of the world. In addition to finding authentic ethnic cuisine from numerous countries, flavours from many regions are showing up on the menus of restaurants across the country. Innovative chefs adapt ethnic recipes and incorporate flavours and ingredients from all over the world into their cooking. Large grocery stores now stock many products that, just a few years ago, would have required a trip to an ethnic market or specialty store.

Despite the incorporation of international flavours into our cooking, regional food is still important to Canadians—cod in Newfoundland and Labrador, seafood in the Maritimes, tourtière and sugar pie in Quebec, the fruits, vegetables and wine of the Niagara region of Ontario, the berries, wheat and beef of the Prairies, the salmon and crab of British Columbia and the arctic char of the Far North.

In addition to the food brought by new arrivals to this country, Canadian food is tied to the bounty of the land, sea, lakes and rivers. The recipes in this book focus mainly on using local products from each region as well as some traditional recipes. Enjoy them whenever the ingredients are available, and may the flavours transport you across this great country.

Farm in Park Corner, PEI

CANADA

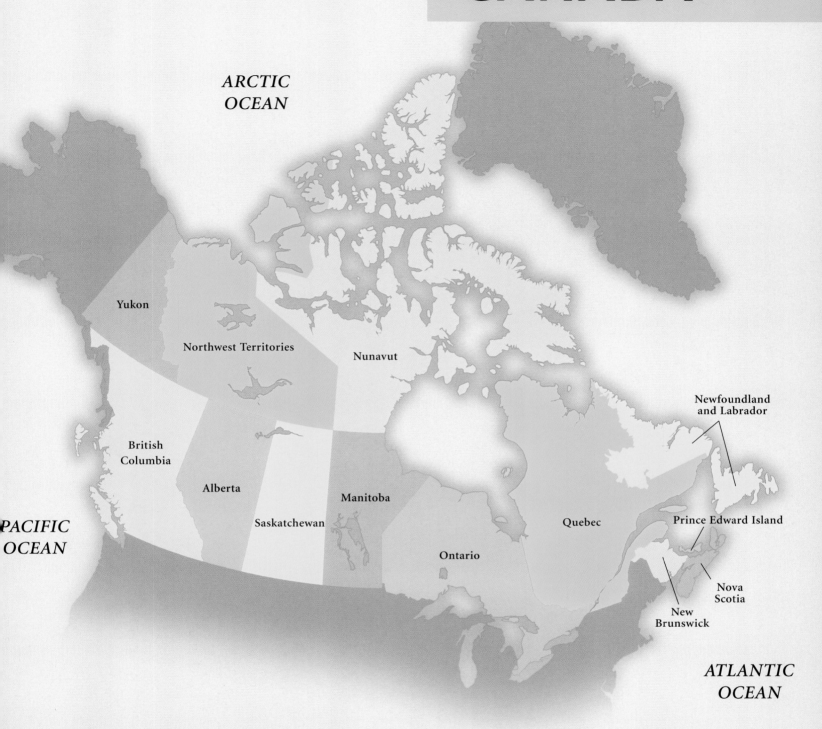

ARCTIC
OCEAN

Yukon

Northwest Territories

Nunavut

Newfoundland
and Labrador

British
Columbia

Alberta

Manitoba

Saskatchewan

Quebec

Prince Edward Island

Ontario

Nova
Scotia

New
Brunswick

PACIFIC
OCEAN

ATLANTIC
OCEAN

Windmills, Pincher Creek, Alberta

NEWFOUNDLAND and LABRADOR

Newfoundland and Labrador is a land of natural beauty, a long history, and friendly people.

Trinity Harbour

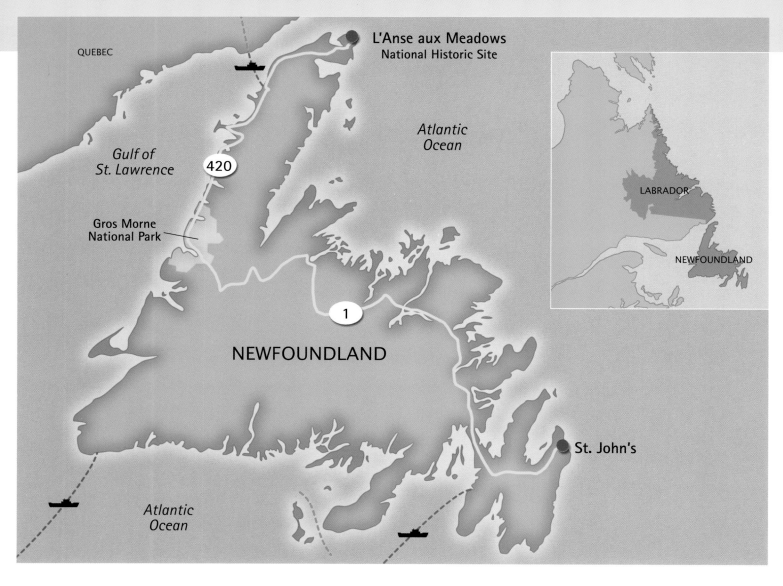

NEWFOUNDLAND AND LABRADOR

Though it was the last province to join Canada (in 1949), Newfoundland is home to the first European settlements in North America. Vikings arrived around 1000 A.D., followed by John Cabot in 1497. And European fishermen—Basques, Spaniards, French and Portuguese—had been visiting the shores of Newfoundland for centuries.

Newfoundland (commonly referred to as "The Rock") and Labrador have much to offer to adventure-seekers: whale watching and iceberg watching as well as the breathtaking fjords of Labrador. The province is a great place for hunting and fishing, and the bounty from these activities—fish and game—forms the basis of Newfoundland and Labrador cuisine.

REGIONAL SPECIALTIES

Look for the Taste of Newfoundland and Labrador logo in restaurants when looking for traditional cuisine.

Cod – Cod was incredibly plentiful around the coast of Newfoundland and for centuries it was the mainstay of the Newfoundland economy. It was preserved by being salted and dried. However, this important resource has been dwindling in numbers and a moratorium was declared in 1992.

Bakeapples or cloudberries – These berries resemble golden-yellow raspberries. Though you won't likely find them fresh, if you see a jar of cloudberry jam, be sure to scoop it up!

Game – The people of Newfoundland and Labrador eat more game than the residents of any other province.

The Spirits of Newfoundland and Labrador

Screech – In exchange for salt cod, Jamaica traded rum with Newfoundland. The story of how this rum earned its name is as follows: An American serviceman during World War II copied a Newfoundlander who downed his rum in one gulp, and he proceeded to emit a bloodcurdling cry. When someone pounded on the door asking what the screech was all about, the answer was, "The screech? 'Tis the rum, me son."

Iceberg Vodka – This award-winning vodka is made from naturally pure iceberg water and spirits made from Ontario corn. A truly Canadian vodka.

Wineries – Newfoundland and Labrador have several wineries specializing in fruit wines made mostly from the berries that are plentiful in this region.

So you want to be an honorary Newfie? Get ready to kiss the fish. The ceremony is called a Screech-In. First, you kiss a cod, then you down some Screech, and then you shout "Long may your big jib draw!"

Gros Morne National Park

St. John's

St. John's was founded in 1528. It is the oldest city in Canada and in all of North America. It was named for the feast day of St. John the Baptist, held on June 24, the day on which John Cabot first sailed into St. John's harbour.

On the eastern coast of Newfoundland, St. John's is the most easterly city in North America. It is the main commercial and financial centre of the province. Steeped in culture and history, it is a destination not to be missed.

What to See and Do

Signal Hill — If you're in St. John's, before hitting the restaurants or pubs, visit Signal Hill. In 1901, Marconi received the first wireless trans-Atlantic message here. This historical site also provides a wonderful view of the city and the sea.

Water Street — When you want a bite to eat, you might want to take a stroll down Water Street, where you will find lots of choices: traditional food, international cuisine or pub fare eaten while listening to music, be it traditional or contemporary.

Quidi Vidi Battery — Visit the Quidi Vidi Battery Provincial Historic Site to learn about the history of the military presence in St. John's over the centuries. Built by the French in 1762, it was later rebuilt by the British, and has now been restored to its 1812 state.

Worth a Detour

Cape Spear – A short drive from St. John's will take you to the most easterly point in North America: Cape Spear. It is home to a National Historic Site as well as the oldest lighthouse in Newfoundland and Labrador.

Gros Morne National Park – On the western coast of Newfoundland is Gros Morne National Park, named a UNESCO World Heritage Site thanks in part to its geological peculiarities. You can experience ice age conditions at the Tablelands. Hikers will be rewarded by spectacular vistas.

L'Anse aux Meadows – If you venture to the northern tip of Newfoundland, you can visit L'Anse aux Meadows National Historic Site, and the remains of a thousand-year-old Viking settlement. At this UNESCO World Heritage Site, you can learn also about the way of life and food of that period.

A picturesque St. John's street

Merritt's Harbour, NF

Lobster and Fish Chowder

6 servings

1 tbsp	butter or margarine	15 mL
1	onion, chopped	1
2	stalks celery, diced	2
2 cups	peeled, diced potato	500 mL
2 cups	water	500 mL
	freshly ground pepper	
1 lb	fresh or frozen fish fillets, cut into 1-inch (2.5 cm) cubes	500 g
3 cups	milk	750 mL
11 oz	cooked or canned lobster meat, drained and cubed	325 g
12 oz	can corn kernels, drained	341 mL
	pinch paprika	
	pinch cayenne pepper (optional)	
	chopped fresh parsley	
3 tbsp	grated Sbrinz or Parmesan cheese	45 mL
3	slices bread, toasted and cubed	3

- Melt butter in a large saucepan; add onion and celery and sauté for 2 to 3 minutes over medium-high heat.
- Add potatoes, water and pepper. Cover and let simmer 10 minutes or until potatoes are nearly tender.
- Add fish cubes, cover and let simmer 5 minutes.
- Add milk and gently stir in lobster meat, corn, paprika and cayenne pepper. Heat over low heat without allowing to boil.
- Garnish with parsley and grated cheese. Serve with croutons.

Hearty Cod Stew

4 servings

4	slices bacon, diced	4
½	red onion, peeled and chopped	½
2	cloves garlic, peeled, crushed and chopped	2
4	potatoes, peeled and diced	4
4 cups	vegetable stock, heated	1 L
2	fresh fennel stalks, chopped	2
	salt and freshly ground pepper	
1½ lbs	fresh cod, rinsed and cubed	750 g
2 tbsp	butter	30 mL
2 tbsp	all-purpose flour	30 mL
1 tbsp	chopped fresh parsley	15 mL

- Cook bacon 6 minutes in a large saucepan over medium heat. Add onion and garlic. Reduce heat to low and cook 4 minutes.
- Stir in potatoes, vegetable stock and fresh fennel. Season well and cook 12 minutes over low heat.
- Add fish and cook 6 minutes. Discard fennel sprigs. Remove 1 cup (250 mL) cooking liquid and set aside.
- Heat butter in separate saucepan over medium heat. Sprinkle in flour and mix well. Cook 15 seconds. Incorporate reserved cooking liquid. Pour mixture into pan containing fish and vegetables; mix gently. Add parsley and serve.

Cod au Gratin

4 servings

1	stalk celery, diced	1
1	carrot, diced	1
1	onion, sliced	1
2	bay leaves	2
	a few parsley sprigs	
	salt and pepper	
4 cups	water	1 L
2 lbs	fresh cod, cut in 4 pieces	1 kg
1½ cups	white sauce, heated	375 mL
1 cup	grated Gruyère cheese	250 mL
	fresh dill, for garnish (optional)	

- Place vegetables and seasonings in sauté pan. Add water and bring to a boil over medium heat.
- Add fish to pan. It should be covered completely by liquid. Cook 8 minutes over low heat.
- Use a slotted spoon to remove fish from pan and drain well. Transfer fish to buttered ovenproof baking dish. Pour white sauce over fish and top with grated cheese.
- Place in oven and broil 5 minutes. Garnish with fresh dill before serving.

Newfoundland coast

Venison and Beer Stew

4 servings

1 tbsp	oil	15 mL
1½ lbs	venison, cubed	750 g
1	large carrot, grated	1
1	stalk celery, finely sliced	1
½ cup	fresh or canned mushrooms	125 mL
1	medium onion, diced	1
1	large green onion, chopped	1
	salt and pepper	
	pinch of paprika	
	chopped parsley	
1	12-oz (340 mL) bottle of beer	1
2 tbsp	cornstarch	30 mL
¼ cup	cold water	50 mL
	toasted croutons	

- Preheat oven to 375ºF (190ºC).
- In a skillet, heat oil and sear venison cubes over high heat.
- Place meat in a casserole dish, add all other ingredients except cold water, cornstarch and croutons. Cover and braise in oven for 45 minutes.
- About 5 minutes before the meat is done, dissolve the cornstarch in cold water, pour over the meat and stir.
- When done, sprinkle with croutons and serve.

Moose Roast

6 to 8 servings

1 lb	salt pork or bacon	500 g
4 lb	moose rump roast	2 kg
1 tbsp	dry mustard	15 mL
2 tsp	salt	10 mL
1 tsp	pepper	5 mL
2	medium onions, sliced	2
2	medium carrots, diced	2
2	stalks celery, diced	2
2 cups	tomatoes, seeded, chopped and strained	500 mL

- Wrap the salt pork or bacon around the roast and refrigerate overnight or 10 to 12 hours. This step will adjust the gamey odor of the meat.
- Preheat oven to 300ºF (150ºC).
- Remove and discard the pork or bacon. Rub the moose thoroughly with dry mustard, salt and pepper.
- Place the moose in a roasting pan surrounded with the onions, carrots, celery and tomatoes.
- Cover and bake for 2 hours for medium doneness. If you prefer your meat well done, roast for an additional 35 to 45 minutes.
- Remove the roast from the oven and slice thin. Serve.

Roast Rabbit

6 servings

If hare is available, by all means, use it instead of the rabbit.

1	4-lb (2 kg) rabbit	1
	salt and pepper	
½ cup	Dijon mustard	125 mL
6 tbsp	butter	90 mL
2 tbsp	flour	30 mL
1½ cups	warm chicken stock	375 mL
2 tbsp	wine vinegar	30 mL
1	bay leaf	1
2 tbsp	fresh tarragon or 1½ tsp (7 mL) dried	30 mL

- Preheat oven to 375°F (190°C).
- Rinse rabbit under cold running water, and then dry well with paper towels.
- Season rabbit with salt and pepper. Brush it with mustard, inside and out.
- Melt 3 tbsp (45 mL) of the butter in a large ovenproof Dutch oven over high heat. When butter is very hot, brown rabbit evenly all over. Continue cooking in oven, uncovered, for 60 minutes.
- In the meantime, prepare the sauce. Melt remaining butter in a small saucepan. Add flour and cook for 2 to 3 minutes over low heat. Stir constantly.
- Gradually stir in chicken stock. Mix in wine vinegar, bay leaf, tarragon, salt and pepper. Simmer for 10 minutes, stirring occasionally.
- Approximately 15 minutes before the rabbit is done, pour the sauce over the rabbit and return to the oven. Continue cooking uncovered.
- To test if the rabbit is done, insert a trussing needle or fork along the inside of the thigh. If no liquid is apparent, the rabbit is cooked.
- Place rabbit on a serving tray. Strain sauce into a gravy boat. Correct seasoning if necessary and serve.

Bakeapple Jam Roll

6 servings

You won't find bakeapples (or cloudberries) at the grocery store, but if you can get your hands on some bakeapple jam, be sure to give this roll a try.

½ cup	icing sugar	125 mL
3	eggs	3
⅓ cup	all-purpose flour	75 mL
2 tbsp	sugar	30 mL
½ cup	cloudberry jam	125 mL
	custard sauce	
	mint leaves	

- Preheat oven to 375ºF (190ºC). Grease and lightly flour a 9 x 13-inch (23 x 33 cm) baking pan.
- Beat together icing sugar and eggs with an electric beater or food processor until pale and frothy.
- Gradually stir in flour with a rubber spatula. Spread batter in prepared pan and bake 10 minutes.
- Meanwhile, cut a piece of waxed paper the same size as the pan and sprinkle sugar evenly over it. Carefully turn the cake upside-down on the waxed paper to unmould. Let cool a few minutes.

- Spread jam evenly over cake. Roll cake gently, starting at one of the short ends. Do not slice cake until it has cooled completely. Serve with custard sauce and mint leaves.

Rum Fritters

Use Newfoundland screech instead of regular rum if you can get it.

¾ cup	raisins	175 mL
⅔ cup	rum	150 mL
1½	envelopes instant yeast	1½
½ cup	warm water	125 mL
4 cups	all-purpose flour	1 L
¼ cup	sugar	50 mL
	pinch of salt	
	grated rind of one lemon	
⅓ cup	chopped walnuts	75 mL
	pinch of cinnamon	
⅓ cup	candied fruit peel	75 mL
	oil for deep frying	
	sugar	

- Soak the raisins in the rum until plump. Dissolve the yeast in the warm water and allow to sit for about 10 minutes, or until foamy.
- Sift the flour into a warm mixing bowl and make a well in the centre. Add the yeast, sugar, salt, lemon rind, walnuts, raisins, rum, cinnamon and candied fruit. Mix thoroughly with a wooden spoon. Add a bit of water if necessary.
- Cover the bowl with a warm cloth and let stand in a warm place for 4 hours or until the dough has doubled.
- Punch the dough down and knead until very smooth. Add water to make the dough easier to work with if necessary.
- Heat the cooking oil in a deep-fryer to 350ºF (180ºC). Gently drop in spoonfuls of dough. Remove from the oil when golden brown. Drain on a paper towel and sprinkle with sugar or icing sugar. Serve.

The MARITIMES

The three smallest provinces—Nova Scotia, Prince Edward Island and New Brunswick— have a lot to offer.

Peggy's Cove, Nova Scotia

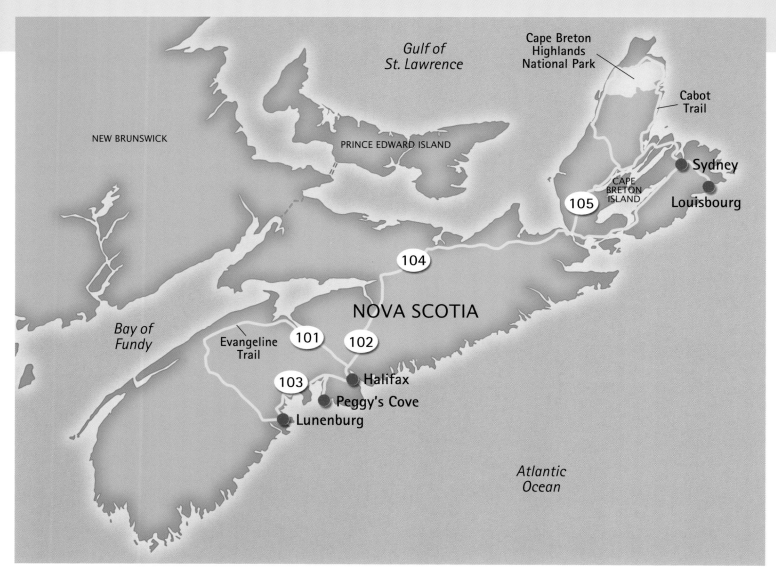

NOVA SCOTIA

One of the founding provinces of Canada, Nova Scotia has historical, cultural and natural interest for everyone. It was home to the Acadians, and the effect of the early French presence is still felt in certain areas. Later immigration brought the Scottish, Irish and British, as well as other Europeans, all contributing to the culture and cuisine of the province.

The farthest you can get from the sea anywhere in Nova Scotia is 56 km (35 miles), so the seaside, whether beach or cliffs, is always a popular destination. But there are other things to do in Nova Scotia; on the next page are some places that shouldn't be missed.

Cabot Trail, Cape Breton

What to See and Do

Cape Breton – No trip to Nova Scotia would be complete without a visit to Cape Breton, for its spectacular views of land and sea as well as its musical legacy. Be sure to drive along the renowned Cabot Trail and visit the National Park and the Louisbourg National Historic Site, the largest historical reconstruction in North America.

Evangeline Trail – Along the shore of the Bay of Fundy lies the Evangeline Trail, named for Longfellow's epic poem, Evangeline, about the deportation of the Acadians. Follow this route through the Annapolis Valley, visiting local artisans and craftspeople.

Halifax – This university town has a lot to offer: historical sites, cultural events, and fine dining. Though smaller than other major Canadian cities, it is cosmopolitan and vibrant. The Halifax Citadel National Historic Site will give you a taste of the city's heritage.

Peggy's Cove – On the south shore of the province lies Peggy's Cove. It may be the most photographed site in Canada, and with good reason. The picturesque fishing village is known for its lighthouse perched atop some rocky boulders.

REGIONAL SPECIALTIES

When eating out, look for the Taste of Nova Scotia logo to be sure you are getting authentic Nova Scotia food.

Annapolis Valley – The sunniest region of Nova Scotia is known for its apple production, but it also produces pears, peaches, plums and corn.

Cape Breton's Glenora Distillery – If you like scotch, you shouldn't miss this. The Glenora distillery is the only one in North America to produce single malt whisky.

Lunenburg – Formally established in 1753, Lunenburg was the first British colonial settlement in Nova Scotia after Halifax. The first settlers were largely from Germany, and this heritage lives on today. The descendants of these settlers have combined traditional cooking with local ingredients to create a cuisine all its own. Solomon Gundy (pickled herring) is a local specialty of German origin. Old Lunenburg has been designated a UNESCO World Heritage Site.

Citadel Hill, Halifax

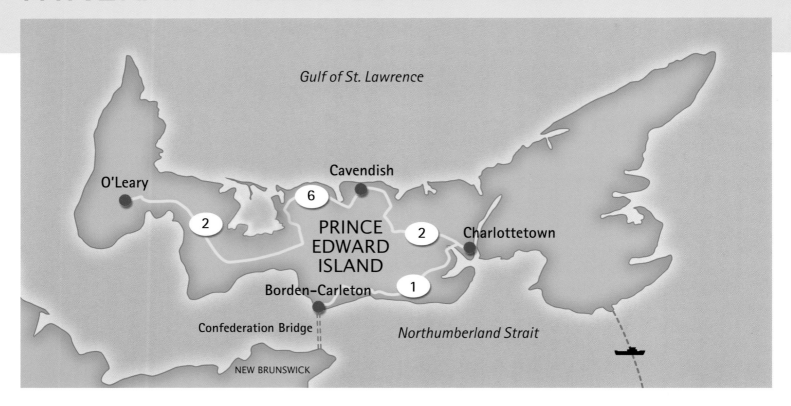

PRINCE EDWARD ISLAND

Prince Edward Island is more than just the home of its world-famous fictional citizen, Anne of Green Gables. And though it is the smallest province in the country, it has big appeal.

Though Charlottetown hosted the talks that led to the creation of the Dominion of Canada, Prince Edward Island didn't join confederation in 1867. Instead, it joined six years later, in 1873. The island's role in the creation of Canada is recorded in the name of the Confederation Bridge.

Cavendish Beach, Prince Edward Island

What to See and Do

Charlottetown – No visit to PEI will be complete without a trip to the capital and largest city. Be sure to check out Peake's Wharf where you can walk along boardwalks, take a boat tour, shop for crafts or grab a bite and one of the many restaurants.

Cavendish – If you are an Anne fan, you can visit Green Gables, the farmhouse that was the setting for L.M. Montgomery's Anne of Green Gables. The various buildings recreate the settings found in the book.

Confederation Bridge – If you drive to PEI, you will probably get to Canada's smallest province by driving over the world's longest bridge over ice-covered waters. This 12.9 km (8 mile) feat of engineering was opened to the public in 1997 to take people and goods to and from the island.

Golf – Though the island is only 195 km (121 miles) from one end to the other, there are more than two dozen golf courses! Some overlook the ocean and all are beautiful. In general, golfing is quite accessible to tourists.

Beaches – With the warmest ocean north of the Carolinas and an irregular coastline with lots of bays and inlets, Prince Edward Island has beaches for every taste.

REGIONAL SPECIALTIES

Culinary Institute of Canada – Charlottetown is home to the Culinary Institute of Canada, one of the most highly regarded cooking schools in the country. It has been training innovative chefs for over 20 years.

Potatoes – It's hard to think of PEI without thinking of potatoes. The island's climate and red soil provide ideal conditions for growing these terrific tubers. To learn more about this culinary staple, visit the Potato Hall of Fame and the PEI Potato Museum (in O'Leary).

Lobster – Although seafood of all kinds abounds on Prince Edward Island, lobster gets top honours. Lobster suppers are organized by restaurants and community groups.

Malpeque Oysters – On the northern coast of PEI lies Malpeque Bay, where renowned malpeque oysters are harvested.

If you want to combine two of the island's food specialties in one, try lobster-stuffed potatoes.

Hay bales, Park Corner, PEI

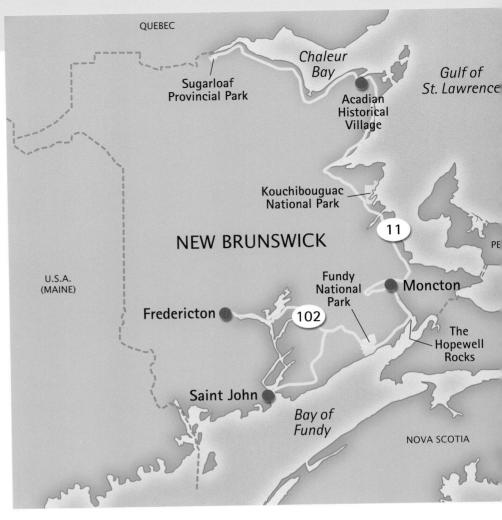

NEW BRUNSWICK

Canada's only officially bilingual province enjoys a delightful mixed heritage provided by its Aboriginal, Acadian and Loyalist roots.

New Brunswick is one of Canada's founding provinces, but its history goes much further back than 1867. The Acadian population was deported in 1755, and after the American Revolution, British Loyalists left the United States to settle in Acadia, preferring to live under British rule. But before any European settlers arrived, the land was home to the Mi'kmaq, Maliseet and Passamaquoddy.

Though forestry is one of the main industries in New Brunswick, the coast is essential to the province's tourism, from the frigid waters of the Bay of Fundy to the warm shores of the Acadian coast. Its capital, Fredericton, is inland.

Acadian village

Places to visit

Bay of Fundy – The highest tides in the world leave their mark on the southern coast of the province. You can appreciate them at beautiful Fundy National Park as well as other sites along the coast.

Kouchibouguac National Park – If you prefer sun, sand and swimming to high tides and cold water, this National Park on the Acadian coast is the place for you.

The Tidal Bore – Twice a day, the tides in the bay of Fundy push the waters of the Petitcodiac river back, towards Moncton. The river appears to flow backwards, at speeds of up to 13 km/h (8 mph).

Moncton – Stop in Acadia's urban capital before continuing north, along the Acadian coast. Visit the Moncton Market for produce, baked goods and crafts, and Magnetic Hill, where your car will mysteriously appear to coast uphill.

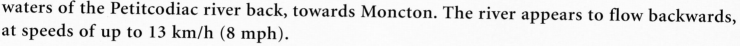

REGIONAL SPECIALTIES

Fiddleheads – In the spring, the young, tightly coiled fronds of the ostrich fern are collected from the forest and turned into a delicious side dish. They are in season for a very short time, so get them while you can!

Dulse – This delicacy is a purple seaweed that is dried and used in soups and stews, though some locals like it best on its own, as a snack eaten out of hand.

St. John City Market – Whether you are looking for fruits and vegetables right from the farm, fish straight from the ocean, or bread fresh from the oven, you'll find it at the St. John City Market, along with lots of other fresh food and local food finds.

A visit to New Brunswick just wouldn't be complete without a taste of Acadian cuisine.

Bay of Fundy

Super Simple Clam Chowder

4 servings

*You can replace the clams with other shellfish if you like.
Or use 12 oz (360 g) of canned clams (with their juice)
if fresh are not available.*

³/₄ cup	white wine	175 mL
36	fresh clams, scrubbed	36
	salt and pepper	
1 tbsp	butter or margarine	15 mL
1	onion, chopped	1
2	carrots, chopped	2
2	potatoes, peeled and diced	2
1 cup	water	250 mL
2 cups	milk	500 mL

- Place the wine and clams in a large skillet. Season with salt and pepper and bring to a boil. Cook, covered, for about 4 minutes over medium heat. Chop clams, discarding any that have not opened. Reserve ½ cup of cooking liquid.
- Melt butter in a large saucepan and sauté vegetables 5 minutes, stirring.
- Add clams and reserved cooking liquid. Add enough of the water to cover ingredients. Let simmer over medium heat until vegetables are tender and liquid has reduced by half (about 15 minutes).
- Add milk and bring just to a boil, stirring constantly. Do not let it come to a full boil. As soon as the mixture starts to bubble, lower heat to keep soup barely simmering as long as possible (3 to 4 minutes).
- Adjust seasoning and serve.

Seared Scallops

4 servings

*Don't overcook scallops, or they will become rubbery.
If you use frozen scallops, do not thaw before cooking.*

¼ cup	all-purpose flour	50 mL
1 tbsp	chopped fresh tarragon	15 mL
	pinch ground white pepper	
1 lb	scallops	500 g
2 tbsp	vegetable oil	30 mL
3	tomatoes, peeled, seeded and diced	3
¼ tsp	garlic salt	1 mL
2	green onions, finely chopped	2
	salt and pepper	

- In a bowl, combine flour, tarragon and white pepper. Toss scallops in flour and shake off excess.
- Heat oil in a nonstick skillet. Add scallops and fry on both sides over medium-high heat just until interior is no longer translucent. Remove scallops from skillet.
- In the same skillet, cook tomatoes, garlic salt and green onions for 10 minutes over medium heat. Season to taste with salt and pepper. Serve scallops on a bed of tomato sauce.

Smoked Salmon on Potato Pancakes

4 servings

*Enjoy both the taste of the sea and PEI potatoes with this
simple dish. It can be served as an appetizer or alongside
a salad as a main meal.*

4	large potatoes	4
1	onion, grated	1
3 tbsp	flour	45 mL
	salt and pepper	
1	large egg, separated	1
2 tbsp	olive oil	30 mL
16	thin slices smoked salmon	16
	sour cream	

- Peel and grate potatoes. Place grated potatoes in a large bowl and cover with cold water. Let stand 15 minutes and then drain well. Squeeze out excess liquid from potatoes.
- Place potatoes in the bowl of an electric mixer. Add onion and flour and season. Mix well. Add egg yolk and mix again.
- Beat the egg white lightly and incorporate into mixture.
- Shape mixture into small pancakes. Refrigerate for one hour.
- Heat half of the oil in a nonstick frying pan over medium heat. Add half of the potato pancakes and cook for 5 minutes on each side. Season well. Remove pancakes from pan and keep hot in oven. Add remaining oil and repeat procedure for remaining pancakes.
- Roll slices of salmon and serve on potato pancakes. Serve with sour cream.

Oysters Remique

6 servings

½ cup	chili sauce	125 mL
½ cup	horseradish	125 mL
2 cups	grated old Canadian cheddar	500 mL
36	oysters	36
2 cups	fine breadcrumbs	500 mL
	fennel fronds or dill (optional)	

- Preheat oven to 450ºF (230ºC).
- Combine the chili sauce and horseradish.
- Shuck and drain the oysters. Discard the flat upper shell and detach the flesh.
- Spoon 1 tsp (5 mL) chili sauce mixture over each oyster. Divide the cheese among the oysters. Top with breadcrumbs and bake in oven until cheese has browned.
- Garnish with fennel or dill and serve.

Sautéed Fiddleheads

4 servings

Fiddleheads must be cooked thoroughly to eliminate the toxic substance they are thought to contain. Before cooking, put them in a plastic bag and shake well to remove any brown scales.

	salt	
2 cups	fiddleheads	500 mL
2 tbsp	butter	30 mL
2	cloves garlic, minced	2
	pepper	
	lemon juice, to taste	

- In a large saucepan, blanch fiddleheads in salted boiling water for 10 minutes. Drain.
- Melt butter in a skillet and add garlic; stir. Add fiddleheads and sauté for 3 minutes. Season with salt and pepper and sprinkle with lemon juice. Serve.

Nova Scotia-Style Paella

4 to 6 servings

This is a great dish for savouring lots of maritime seafood.

8	mussels, cleaned	8
8	clams, cleaned	8
	pepper	
2 lbs	chicken, cut into serving pieces and trimmed of fat	1 kg
¼ cup	vegetable oil	50 mL
2	cloves garlic, coarsely chopped	2
1	onion, coarsely chopped	1
1	red pepper, cut into strips	1
2	squid, cleaned out and cut into pieces (optional)	2
2 tsp	paprika	10 mL
1 cup	fresh or frozen peas	250 mL
2 cups	raw long-grain rice	500 mL
4 cups	chicken stock	1 L
¼ tsp	saffron threads, soaked in a little water	1 mL
¼ lb	large cooked shrimp	125 g
	meat of 1 cooked lobster, cut in pieces	
	pepper	

- Cook mussels and clams in a little boiling water until shells open. Drain and set aside, discarding any unopened shellfish.
- Sprinkle chicken pieces with pepper.
- Heat oil in a large casserole or baking dish and brown chicken all over. Add garlic, onion, red pepper and squid. Stir well and cook until onion is tender.
- Sprinkle in paprika. Add peas and then slowly pour in rice, stirring. Cook, stirring constantly, until rice is golden.
- In a saucepan, bring chicken stock to a boil. Pour over rice mixture. Add saffron, stir well and cook over very high heat for about 5 minutes.
- Add mussels, clams, shrimp and lobster. Lower heat, cover and cook another 10 minutes without stirring. The rice should be done when it has absorbed all the liquid.
- Let stand 5 minutes before serving.

Mussels in Creamy White Wine Sauce

4 servings

6 lbs	fresh mussels, washed, scrubbed and bearded	3 kg
3	shallots, finely chopped	3
2 tbsp	chopped fresh parsley	30 mL
2 tbsp	chopped fresh chervil	30 mL
¾ cup	dry white wine	175 mL
2 tbsp	butter	30 mL
	freshly ground pepper	
½ cup	heavy cream (35% MF)	125 mL
½	red bell pepper, finely chopped	½

- Place mussels in a large pot. Add shallots, fresh herbs, wine and butter; mix well. Season with pepper, cover and cook over low heat until shells open. Shake pot several times during cooking.
- With a slotted spoon, transfer mussels to a bowl, discarding any unopened mussels. Continue cooking liquid until reduced by half. Add cream and bring to a boil. Reduce heat to low, add red pepper and mussels and simmer 3 minutes. Serve immediately.

Salmon with Sorrel Sauce

4 servings

1 tbsp	olive oil	15 mL
1 tbsp	butter or margarine	15 mL
4	thick salmon fillets, about 7 oz (200 g) each	4
¼ cup	chopped fresh sorrel	50 mL
¼ cup	dry white wine	50 mL
¼ cup	light cream cheese	50 mL
¼ cup	skim milk	50 mL
2 tbsp	fresh lemon juice	30 mL
	freshly ground pepper	

- Preheat oven to 350ºF (180ºC). Heat oil and butter in an ovenproof skillet over medium heat. Add salmon and cook for 5 minutes on each side. Stir in sorrel and white wine. Cover and bake for 10 minutes.
- Remove salmon from pan and keep warm. Over low heat, simmer pan juices. Gradually whisk in cream cheese and then milk. Stir in lemon juice and season to taste.
- Pour sorrel sauce on heated plates and arrange salmon on top.

Lobster Newburg

4 servings

1½ cups	dry white wine	375 mL
½ cup	clam juice	125 ml
2	1½-lb (750 g) boiled lobsters	2
4 tbsp	butter	60 mL
4	shallots, peeled and chopped	4
	freshly ground pepper	
	paprika to taste	
¾ lb	fresh mushrooms, cleaned and diced	350 g
2 tbsp	all-purpose flour	30 mL
1 cup	light cream, heated	250 mL
¼ cup	Madeira wine	50 mL
	salt	
	chopped fresh parsley	

- Bring white wine to a boil in a saucepan and cook 3 minutes. Add clam juice and reduce heat to low. Simmer until ready to use.
- Split lobsters in half lengthwise. Discard intestinal sac. Scoop out any tomalley and coral and reserve in a small bowl. Remove lobster meat from shells and dice large; set aside.
- Rinse shells and dry in warm oven.
- Heat butter in a frying pan over medium heat. Add lobster meat, shallots, pepper and paprika. Cook for 2 minutes over high heat. Remove lobster from pan and set aside.
- Add mushrooms to pan and season well. Cook 4 minutes over medium heat. Sprinkle in flour and mix well; cook for 2 minutes.
- Incorporate simmering wine mixture to mushrooms. Stir well and pour in cream. Season, stir and cook sauce for 6 minutes over low heat.
- Stir in reserved tomalley and coral. Return lobster to pan and stir in Madeira wine. Season well and simmer for 4 minutes.
- Fill lobster shells with mixture and sprinkle with parsley. Serve.

Hopewell Rocks, NB

Rappie Pie

4 to 6 servings

This is an adaptation of a traditional Acadian dish.

1	3-lb (1.5 kg) chicken	1
2 lbs	potatoes	1 kg
2 tbsp	olive oil	30 mL
2 tbsp	butter	30 mL
1	large onion, chopped	1
1	clove garlic, minced	1
1½ cups	chicken stock	375 mL
	salt and freshly ground pepper	
½ cup	breadcrumbs	125 mL
½ cup	grated Parmesan cheese	125 mL

- Place the chicken in a large pot with enough water to cover. Bring to a boil. Reduce heat and simmer until thoroughly cooked, about 1 hour.
- While chicken is simmering, peel the potatoes and add to the pot with the chicken. Cook for about 30 to 45 minutes, or until just cooked through. Remove from pot and mash.
- In a large skillet, melt the butter and add the oil. Add the onion and sauté for about 5 minutes. Add the garlic and mashed potatoes. Add the chicken stock and mix together well to create a firm purée. Season to taste.
- When the chicken is cooked, cut it into large pieces. In a small bowl, mix together the breadcrumbs and the Parmesan cheese.
- Preheat oven to 350ºF (180ºC).
- Butter a large baking dish. Cover the bottom with half of the potato mixture. Cover the potatoes with the chicken. Cover with the remaining potatoes. Sprinkle the breadcrumb mixture evenly over top.
- Bake for 45 minutes or until the top is golden.

Woodstock, NB

Fish and Seafood Pie

4 servings

4 cups	fish stock	1 L
2	potatoes, cubed	2
4	carrots, halved and sliced	4
2	leeks, white part only, sliced	2
½ lb	fresh scallops	250 g
½ lb	fresh cod	250 g
3 tbsp	butter	45 mL
3 tbsp	all-purpose flour	45 mL
3	cloves garlic, minced	3
2 tbsp	chopped fresh parsley	30 mL
	salt and freshly ground pepper	
½ lb	fresh crabmeat	250 g
1 cup	peas	250 mL
½ lb	shortcrust pastry	250 g
1	egg yolk, beaten	1

- Pour fish stock into a large saucepan and bring to a boil; add potatoes and cook 5 minutes. Add carrots and leek; continue cooking 5 minutes. Remove vegetables and set aside.
- Poach scallops and cod in simmering fish stock for 2 minutes. Remove and set aside.
- Preheat oven to 400ºF (200ºC).
- Melt butter in another saucepan, add flour and cook 1 minute over low heat. With a whisk, blend in fish stock and bring to a boil, stirring constantly until thick. Add garlic and parsley; season well.
- Return vegetables, cod, and scallops to sauce; add crabmeat and peas. Mix well and transfer to an ovenproof dish.
- Roll out pastry to cover the dish. Cut 2 openings in pastry to allow the steam to escape, and brush the surface with the egg yolk. Bake for about 35 minutes, or until pastry is golden.

Strawberry-Rhubarb Pie

6 to 8 servings

	pastry for double pie crust	
1 cup	sugar	250 mL
½ cup	brown sugar	125 mL
⅓ cup	all-purpose flour	75 mL
3 cups	rhubarb, cut in 1-inch	750 mL
	(2.5 cm) lengths	
1 cup	strawberries, quartered	250 mL
	icing sugar (optional)	
	crème fraîche or whipped cream	

- Preheat oven to 450°F (230°C).
- Roll out half the pastry and line a 9-inch (22 cm) pie plate with it.
- In a large bowl, stir together the sugar, brown sugar and flour. Stir in the rhubarb and strawberries. Fill the pie plate with the fruit mixture. Cover with the remaining pastry, rolled out thin. Seal the edges and cut slits in the pastry or a make a small hole in the centre.
- Bake for 15 minutes. Reduce the heat to 375°F (190°C) and continue baking for 40 to 45 minutes.
- Remove the pie from the oven and sprinkle with icing sugar if desired. Let cool partially before serving. Serve with a dollop of crème fraîche or whipped cream.

Blueberry Grunt

8 servings

*This east-coast dessert is basically dumplings cooked
in a delicious blueberry sauce.*

Sauce

½ cup	orange juice	125 mL
1 tbsp	lime juice	15 mL
½ cup	maple syrup	125 mL
½ cup	white sugar	125 mL
½ tsp	nutmeg	2 mL
5 cups	fresh blueberries	1.25 L

Dumplings

3 cups	flour	750 mL
4 tsp	baking powder	20 mL
½ tsp	salt	2 mL
1 tbsp	brown sugar	15 mL
	dash cinnamon	
4 tbsp	unsalted butter	60 mL
½ cup	heavy cream (35% MF)	125 mL
½ cup	milk	125 mL

- In a wide saucepan, bring the orange juice and lemon juice to a boil Add the maple syrup, sugar, nutmeg and blueberries and let simmer for about 10 minutes.

- Meanwhile, make the dough. Sift the flour into a bowl. Add the baking powder, salt, sugar and cinnamon; stir together. Cut the butter into the dry ingredients. Add the cream and milk; mix to make a soft dough.

- Drop the dough by large spoonfuls into the simmering blueberry mixture. Increase heat slightly, cover and continue simmering for about 20 minutes to obtain puffed dumplings. Serve dumplings with sauce while hot.

QUEBEC

The distinct culture of La Belle Province translates into distinct cuisine, too.

Magdalen Islands

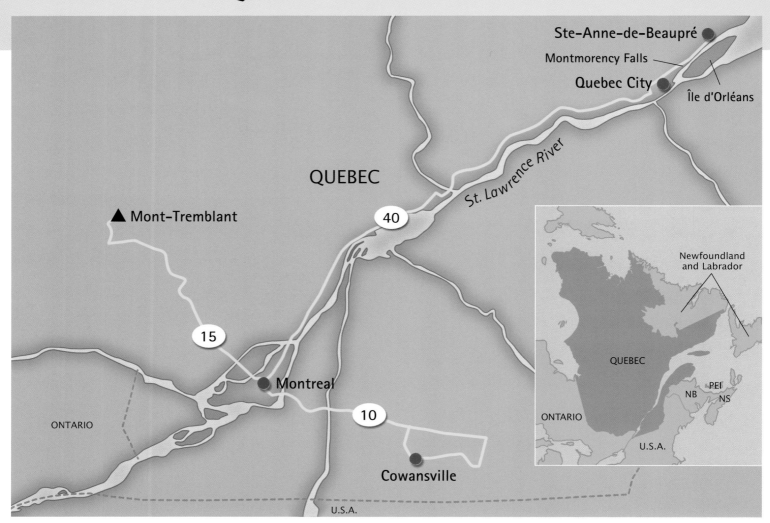

QUEBEC

Quebec's French heritage permeates into most aspects of life. Not only is the language different—Quebec is the only province whose official language is French—but so is the culture, the law (Quebec uses Civil Law, not Common Law) and, of course, the food.

Canada's largest province is by no means homogenous. The various regions provide different geographical, touristic, and culinary offerings: the culture and history of the cities, the cliffs and coast of the Gaspé, the charming villages of Charlevoix and the Eastern Townships, and the vast unspoiled lands of the North.

The main geographical feature of the province is the great St. Lawrence river. It played a central role in the early settlement of the interior of the continent, and continues to be essential to life in Quebec. Close to 80% of the population of Quebec lives in cities and towns along the St. Lawrence.

In Gatineau park

What to See and Do

Every region has something special to offer, but some activities are popular throughout much of the province:

Cycling – The province has an impressive network of bike paths to suit any level of fitness and experience, from short day trips to longer cycling vacations. Over the past few years, various old railway lines have been converted to bike paths, perfect for weekend rides.

Skiing – Though the Laurentian mountains aren't as high as the Rockies, they have their own allure and are very skiable and accessible from Montreal for day trips. The Tremblant resort village on the slopes of Mont Tremblant is world famous.

Fishing – There are many fishing venues to choose from in Quebec, be it any of the thousands of lakes north of the St. Lawrence or any of the rivers, including the St. Lawrence. In the winter, certain lakes are covered in ice fishing huts. One of the most famous fishing spots is the Sainte-Anne river, where every January and February a village of huts is set up and people fish for tommycod, which are swimming upstream to spawn.

REGIONAL SPECIALTIES

Traditional vs. Modern food – In many Quebec families, traditional food is still an important part of certain celebrations, such as Christmas and New Year's. However, you'd generally have a hard time finding foods such as tourtière, pea soup, and other traditional foods in restaurants (though you might have better luck with sugar pie). Top chefs in Quebec put an emphasis on local and regional foods, providing fresh, top-quality cuisine. Among the up-and-coming foods of Quebec is foie gras. Quebec foie gras is recognized for its excellent quality, and is renowned across North America.

Maple Syrup – Quebec produces more maple syrup than any other province. Though it is enjoyed all year long, it takes centre stage in March and April when the sap is flowing and Quebecers get together with family and friends at sugar shacks (*cabanes à sucre*) across the province. There, they eat baked beans, ham, pork rinds, omelets, and more, all served with maple syrup, of course. The meal is finished off with some maple taffy poured on snow (*tire sur neige*).

St-Maurice-de-l'Echourie

Old Quebec viewed from the St. Lawrence

Quebec City

Not only is Quebec City the capital of the province, it is also the oldest city in Quebec. Founded in 1608 by Samuel de Champlain because of its strategic importance, it retains a certain old-world feel. It is located on a rocky cliff overlooking the St. Lawrence river. The old city (*Vieux Québec*) has been designated a UNESCO World Heritage Site.

Winter Wonderland

Though Quebec City is a popular and beautiful destination year-round, winter is a great time of year to visit the provincial capital, as long as you bundle up.

Carnival – The world's biggest winter carnival is the longest running carnival in the world. The focal point is the Ice Palace, and from there visitors can admire the entries in the snow-sculpture competitions. Sculptors from across the country and around the world create temporary masterpieces out of enormous blocks of ice or snow. Parades, dogsled races and tobogganing also take place during the festivities.

Ice Hotel – This hotel made of ice and snow is the coolest place to stay in Quebec City! Guests sleep on a queen size bed covered in a plank of wood, foam, a caribou pelt and a sleeping bag graded to –30ºC (–22ºF). The inside of the hotel is a nippy –5 to –2ºC (23 to 28ºF)—you might want to warm up with a drink at the bar before heading to bed.

Winter Sports – Quebec City has a lot to offer the winter sports enthusiast: cross-country skiing on the Plains of Abraham, skating at Place d'Youville or downhill skiing and snowboarding at any of the several ski resorts in the Greater Quebec City region, such as Mont-Sainte-Anne and the Massif.

Worth a Detour

Montmorency Falls – About 15 minutes east of Quebec City you'll find these falls, the highest in the province and higher than Niagara Falls. To fully appreciate the view, you can reach the top by cable car or you can get some exercise by climbing the 487 stairs.

Île d'Orléans – Across from Montmorency Falls, in the middle of the St. Lawrence, lies Île d'Orléans. It was settled in the beginning of the seventeenth century, and the period architecture is one point of interest. Early settlers took advantage of the fertile soil of the island, and that tradition has continued. Crops include potatoes, apples and strawberries.

Ste-Anne-de-Beaupré – This Catholic shrine is a destination of choice for pious pilgrims from across the country. The ornate Sainte-Anne Basilica welcomes 1.5 million visitors every year.

Local Food

Two historic grocery stores on rue St. Jean are well worth a visit.

W.E. Bégin – This charming hundred-year-old grocery store is also where you can buy renowned Bégin smoked ham. It is prepared according to a traditional procedure in small quantities and is a favourite at Easter.

J.A. Moisan – Founded in 1871, this grocery store is believed to be the oldest in North America. It specializes in fine, often hard-to-find products, which are displayed in a building that dates back to the beginning of the nineteenth century.

Winter in Quebec

Cap-Bon-Ami

Montreal at night

Montreal

The island of Montreal is home to the city of the same name. The island lies at the confluence of the St. Lawrence and Ottawa rivers. It was settled by the French in 1642, eventually named for the mountain at the centre of the island. When New France was ceded to the British, English and Scottish settlers came to Montreal to take advantage of its economic potential, making it an important business centre by 1832.

Montreal is a North American city with a European feel. It is the second largest city in Canada and the second largest French-speaking city in the world. But walking the streets of the city, you are sure to hear more than just French or English. Montreal is home to hundreds of thousands of immigrants—recent and less-so—from around the world. These immigrants brought with them their language, culture and cuisine, enriching the city and making it truly cosmopolitan.

What to See and Do

Churches – Montreal is known for its numerous churches. Some of those worth a visit are the Notre-Dame Basilica, a towering neo-gothic structure dating back to 1829, in its present incarnation, and St. Joseph's Oratory, where the devout still sometimes climb the almost 300 stairs on their knees. The oratory is set on the mountainside, and its huge copper dome can be seen from many kilometres away.

Museums – There are museums for every taste in Montreal, whether you prefer fine arts, architecture or history. The Pointe-à-Callière museum in Old Montreal incorporates the remains of early structures of the city into its underground exhibits.

Nature – You don't need to leave the city to get in tune with nature. Visit Mount Royal in the centre of the island, a vast area of green space that is perfect for walking and picnicking. The Montreal Botanical Garden is one of the largest and most beautiful of its kind in the world. It includes a Japanese Garden, a Chinese Garden and an Aboriginal Garden.

Festivals – Summer is the season of festivals in Montreal. A few of the best known and most popular are the International Jazz Festival, the Just for Laughs comedy festival and the International Fireworks Competition, not to mention the Formula 1 Grand Prix of Canada.

Worth a Detour

Laurentians – The Laurentian mountains begin less than an hour's drive north of Montreal. Skiing, hiking, cycling and golf are just some of the activities available, in addition to admiring the view, especially in autumn.

Eastern Townships – A bit further away, southeast of Montreal, lies this region settled by English loyalists, and it retains a distinct flavour. Brome Lake is renowned for its duck, as well as for the charming town on its shores, Knowlton.

Local Food

Smoked Meat – The meat in question is beef, namely beef brisket, that has been spiced, cured and smoked. It resembles a cross between pastrami and corned beef. Montrealers love a good discussion about the best purveyor in town. Smoked meat appears to be a gift from eastern European Jewish immigrants.

Bagels – The bagels made at traditional bakeries in Montreal are different from those found elsewhere in North America. They are smaller with a bigger hole, and the dough is dense and chewy. They are boiled before being baked in wood-fired ovens.

Public Markets – City dwellers can meet farmers at Jean-Talon, Maisonneuve and Atwater public markets. In addition to fresh produce, you can find butchers, cheese shops, bakeries and a variety of specialty food stores that are open all year long.

Quebec's Fine Cheeses

QUEBEC'S CHEESE INDUSTRY has grown by leaps and bounds over the last few decades. Monks in places such as Oka, Saint-Benoît-du-Lac and Mont-Laurier were among the first cheese producers in the province. Now, Quebec cheeses win awards and are beginning to rival French cheeses in quality and variety.

There are cheeses for every taste, from familiar cheddars to feisty blues and creamy Bries. Choose from fresh cheeses to those aged for several years. Some cheeses are made using traditional methods with only the milk produced by the cheesemaker's herd. Others are made in factories and shipped across the country.

Most of the cheeses produced in Quebec are made from cow's milk, but more and more producers are making wonderful cheese using goat's milk and sheep's milk. All of these types of milk can be made into a great variety of cheeses. The flavour of the cheese depends in part on the type of food eaten by the cows, goats or sheep that produced the milk. Sheep's milk is higher in fat than the others, resulting in a creamier cheese that is generally quite mild tasting. Goat milk can be made into many types of cheese, not just the goat cheese log that comes to mind first when we think of goat cheese.

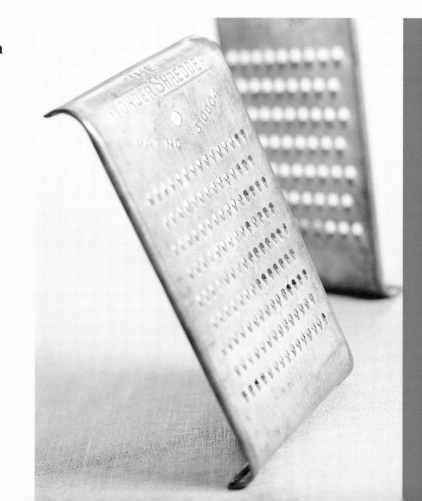

Soft cheeses include such well-known varieties as Brie and Camembert. They generally have a rich creamy texture. The rind can be natural, as are the rinds in this photo, or washed with a briny solution that may include beer, wine or cider to add additional flavour.

Veined cheeses include several varieties of what are commonly called blue cheeses, such as Gorgonzola and Stilton. They can have a variety of textures, from very creamy to quite hard and crumbly.

Firm and hard cheeses include Cheddar, Gouda and Parmesan. Depending on their age and the process used to make them, they can range from a very mild flavour to a more pronounced taste.

Fresh cheeses have undergone the least amount of processing and tend to be quite mild. Cream cheese and cottage cheese, as well as many sorts of goat cheese, belong to this category.

The map on the next few pages identifies many of the cheesemakers in the province.

ABITIBI-TÉMISCAMINGUE

1. **Chèvrerie Dion**
   128 Route 101, Montbaillard – (819) 797-2617 – www3.sympatico.ca/chevreriedion
2. **Le Fromage au village**
   45 Notre-Dame St. West, Lorrainville – (819) 625-2255 –
   www.municipalite.lorrainville.qc.ca/village/villageA.html
3. **La vache à Maillotte**
   604 2nd St. East, La Sarre – (819) 333-1121 – www.abitibi-ouest.net/vache_maillotte.cfm

OUTAOUAIS

4. **La Biquetterie**
   470 Route 315, Chénéville – (819) 428-3061
   www.ville.cheneville.qc.ca/commerces/biquetterie.htm
5. **Ferme Floralpe**
   1700 Route 148, Papineauville – (819) 427-5700
6. **La Trappe à fromage de l'Outaouais**
   200 Bellehumeur St., Gatineau – (819) 243-6411

LAURENTIANS

7. **Agropur, co-op, fine cheese division**
   1400 Oka Road, Oka – (450) 479-6396
8. **Fromagerie du Vieux Saint-François**
   4740 Milles-Îles Blvd., Laval – (450) 666-6810 – www.fromagerieduvieuxstfrancois.com
9. **Fromagerie Le P'tit Train du Nord**
   624 Paquette Blvd., Mont-Laurier – (819) 623-2250 – http://membres.lycos.fr/traindunord
10. **Fromages de l'Érablière**
    1580 Route Eugène-Trinquier, Mont-Laurier – (819) 623-5889 –
    www.fromageduquebec.qc.ca/erabliere.html

LANAUDIÈRE

11. **La Bergère et le Chevrier**
    119 Grande-Côte East, Lanoraie – (450) 887-1979 – www.bergerechevrier.qc.ca
12. **Fromagerie Champêtre**
    415 des Industries Blvd., Le Gardeur – (450) 654-1308
13. **Fromagerie du Champ à la Meule**
    3601 Principale St., Notre-Dame-de-Lourdes – (450) 753-9217
14. **Fromagerie Domaine Féodal inc.**
    1303 Rang Bayonne South, Berthier – (450) 836-7979 or (418) 328-8788 –
    www.tourisme-lanaudiere.qc.ca
15. **Fromagerie La Suisse normande**
    985 Rang Rivière Nord, Saint-Roch-de-l'Achigan – (450) 588-6503
16. **Fromagerie La Voie lactée inc.**
    2815 Route 343, L'Assomption – (450) 588-1080

MAURICIE/PORTNEUF/QUÉBEC

17. **Ferme Caron**
    1091 Saint-Jean, Saint-Louis-de-France – (819) 379-1772
18. **Ferme S.M.A.**
    2222 d'Estimauville St., Beauport – (418) 667-0478
19. **Ferme Tourilli**
    1541 Rang Notre-Dame, Saint-Raymond-de-Portneuf – (418) 337-2876 –
    www.fromageduquebec.qc.ca/tourilli.html
20. **Fromagerie Côte de Beaupré**
    9430 Sainte-Anne Blvd., Sainte-Anne-de-Beaupré –
    (418) 827-1771, 1-888-372-1771
21. **Fromageries Jonathan**
    400 de Lanaudière, Sainte-Anne-de-la-Pérade – (418) 325-3536 –
    www.fromageriesjonathan.com
22. **Saputo**
    500 Rang Saint-Isidore, Saint-Raymond – (418) 337-4287 – www.saputo.com

MONTÉRÉGIE

23. **Agropur, co-op, fine cheese division**
    995 Johnson St., Saint-Hyacinthe – (450) 773-6493
24. **Ferme Diodati**
    1329 Saint-Dominique Rd., Les Cèdres – (450) 452-4249
25. **Ferme Mes Petits Caprices**
    4395 Rang des Étangs, Saint-Jean-Baptiste – (450) 467-3991
26. **Ferme Yogecostere**
    1500 montée Latulippe, Sainte-Justine-de-Newton – (450) 764-3563 (3448)
27. **Fromagerie Au Gré Des Champs**
    400 Rang Saint-Édouard, Saint-Jean-sur-Richelieu – (450) 346-8732 –
    www.fromageduquebec.qc.ca/augredeschamps.html
28. **Fromagerie Clément/Damafro**
    54 Principale St., Saint-Damase – (450) 797-3301 – www.damafro.ca
29. **Fromagerie Fritz Kaiser**
    4th Concession, Noyan –(450) 294-2207
30. **Fromagerie Le Chèvre-Naud**
    Vignoble La Bauge, 155 des Érables, Brigham – (450) 266-2149 – www.labauge.com
31. **Fromagerie Monsieur Jourdain**
    2400 Ridge Rd., Huntingdon – (514) 264-9276
32. **Fromagerie Ruban Bleu**
    449 Rang Saint-Simon, Saint-Isidore-de-Laprairie – (450) 454-4405 – www.rubanbleu.net
33. **Fromages Riviera**
    1040 Fiset Blvd., Sorel-Tracy – (450) 743-0011
34. **Les Produits de Marque Liberté**
    1423 Provencher Blvd., Brossard – (514) 875-3992 – www.liberté.qc.ca

Guide to Quebec's Fine Cheeses

LEGEND:

 Cow

 Sheep

Goat

Shop

Tour available

Abitibi-Témiscamingue

Rouyn-Noranda

Lorrainville

Outaouais

Laurentian

Mont-Laurier

Gatineau

CENTRE-DU-QUÉBEC

35. **Agrilait, Agricultural Cooperative**
    Fromage Saint-Guillaume, 83 de l'Église Rd., Saint-Guillaume – (819) 396-2022 –
    www3.sympatico.ca/agrilait
36. **Bergerie Jeannine**
    134 Rang 10, Saint-Rémi-de-Tingwick – (819) 359-2568
37. **Éco-Délices**
    766 Rang 9 East, Plessisville – (819) 362-7472
38. **Fromage Côté**
    Sales counters: 80 Hôtel-de-Ville St., Warwick – (819) 358-3300
    1245 Forand St., Plessisville – (819) 362-6378
39. **Fromagerie L'Ancêtre**
    1615 Port-Royal Blvd., Saint-Grégoire secteur, City of Bécancour – (819) 233-9157 –
40. **Fomagerie Lemaire**
    2095 Route 122, Saint-Cyrille – (819) 478-0601 – http://fromagerie-lemaire.ca
41. **Fromagerie Tournevent**
    7004 Hince, Chesterville – (819) 382-2208 – www.chevre-tournevent.qc.ca
42. **La Moutonnière**
    Sainte-Hélène-de-Chester – (819) 382-2300 – www.lamoutonniere.ca

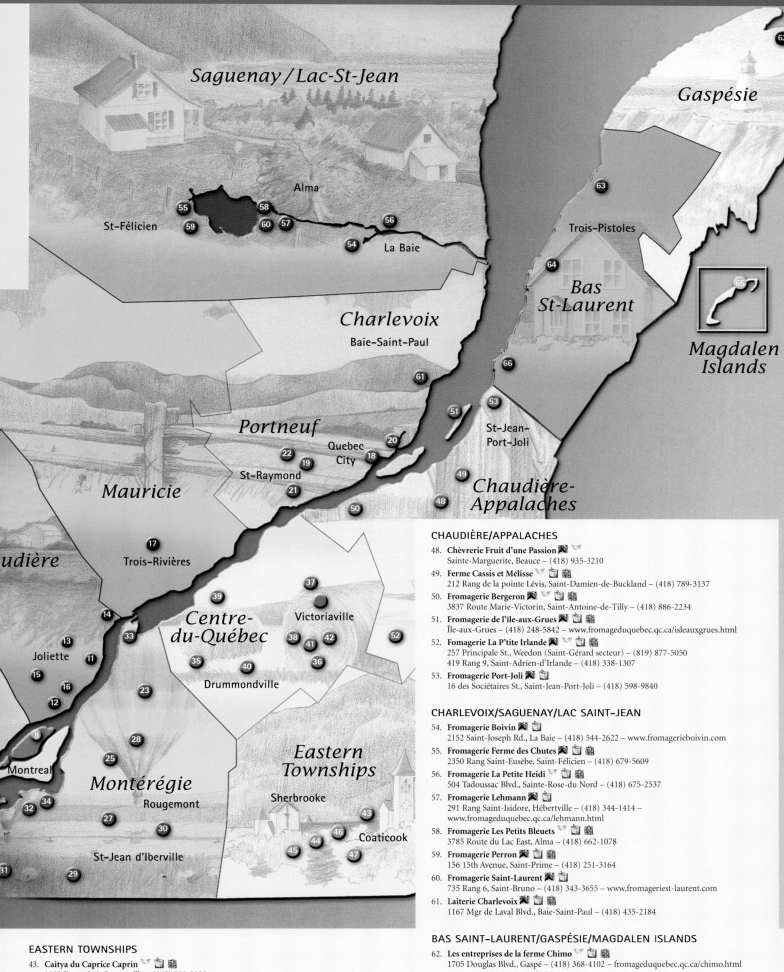

Saguenay / Lac-St-Jean

Alma

55 58
59 60 57
54
56

St-Félicien

La Baie

62

Gaspésie

63

Trois-Pistoles

64

Bas
St-Laurent

65

Magdalen
Islands

Charlevoix

Baie-Saint-Paul

66

61

51 53

St-Jean-
Port-Joli

Portneuf

Quebec
City

22 20
19 18
21

St-Raymond

49

Chaudière-
Appalaches

48

Mauricie

50

17

Trois-Rivières

udière

37

39

14

Centre-
du-Québec

Victoriaville

33

13

38 41 42 52

Joliette

11

35 36

15 16

40

12

Drummondville

23

8

28

Eastern
Townships

25

Montreal

Montérégie

Sherbrooke

32 34

Rougemont

43

27

30

46

44

Coaticook

45 47

St-Jean d'Iberville

31

29

CHAUDIÈRE/APPALACHES

48. **Chèvrerie Fruit d'une Passion**
Sainte-Marguerite, Beauce – (418) 935-3210

49. **Ferme Cassis et Mélisse**
212 Rang de la pointe Lévis, Saint-Damien-de-Buckland – (418) 789-3137

50. **Fromagerie Bergeron**
3837 Route Marie-Victorin, Saint-Antoine-de-Tilly – (418) 886-2234

51. **Fromagerie de l'île-aux-Grues**
Île-aux-Grues – (418) 248-5842 – www.fromageduquebec.qc.ca/isleauxgrues.html

52. **Fomagerie La P'tite Irlande**
257 Principale St., Weedon (Saint-Gérard secteur) – (819) 877-5050
419 Rang 9, Saint-Adrien-d'Irlande – (418) 338-1307

53. **Fromagerie Port-Joli**
16 des Sociétaires St., Saint-Jean-Port-Joli – (418) 598-9840

CHARLEVOIX/SAGUENAY/LAC SAINT-JEAN

54. **Fromagerie Boivin**
2152 Saint-Joseph Rd., La Baie – (418) 544-2622 – www.fromagerieboivin.com

55. **Fromagerie Ferme des Chutes**
2350 Rang Saint-Eusèbe, Saint-Félicien – (418) 679-5609

56. **Fromagerie La Petite Heidi**
504 Tadoussac Blvd., Sainte-Rose-du-Nord – (418) 675-2537

57. **Fromagerie Lehmann**
291 Rang Saint-Isidore, Hébertville – (418) 344-1414 –
www.fromageduquebec.qc.ca/lehmann.html

58. **Fromagerie Les Petits Bleuets**
3785 Route du Lac East, Alma – (418) 662-1078

59. **Fromagerie Perron**
156 15th Avenue, Saint-Prime – (418) 251-3164

60. **Fromagerie Saint-Laurent**
735 Rang 6, Saint-Bruno – (418) 343-3655 – www.fromageriest-laurent.com

61. **Laiterie Charlevoix**
1167 Mgr de Laval Blvd., Baie-Saint-Paul – (418) 435-2184

EASTERN TOWNSHIPS

43. **Caitya du Caprice Caprin**
1023 Route 210, Sawyerville – (819) 889-2958

44. **Ferme Saint-Raphaël**

45. **Fromagerie de l'abbaye de Saint-Benoît-du-Lac**
Saint-Benoît-du-Lac – (819) 843-4080 – www.st-benoit-du-lac.com

46. **Fromagerie La Germaine**
72 Cordon Rd., Sainte-Edwidge-de-Clifton – (819) 849-3238 –
www.produitsdelaferme.com/la-germaine

47. **Laiterie de Coaticook**
1000 Child St., Coaticook – (819) 849-2272 – www.produitsdelaferme.com/laiteriecoaticook

BAS SAINT-LAURENT/GASPÉSIE/MAGDALEN ISLANDS

62. **Les entreprises de la ferme Chimo**
1705 Douglas Blvd., Gaspé – (418) 368-4102 – fromageduquebec.qc.ca/chimo.html

63. **Fromagerie De Lavoye**
224 Route 132 West, Ste-Luce-sur-Mer – (418) 739-4116

64. **Fromagerie des Basques**
69 Route 132 West, Trois-Pistoles – (418) 851-2189 –
www.info-basques.com/gala/fromager.php

65. **Fromagerie du Pied-de-Vent**
Hâvre-aux-Maisons – (418) 969-9292 – www.fromageduquebec.qc.ca/pieddevent.html

66. **Fromagerie Le Mouton Blanc**
176 Route 230 West, La Pocatière – (418) 856-6627

Note: Contact information was correct as of May 2004.
Map © Conseil de l'industrie laitière du Québec inc.

Percé

Split-Pea Soup

4 to 6 servings

2 tbsp	bacon fat	30 mL
1	medium onion, chopped	1
2	stalks celery, diced	2
1	large carrot, diced	1
1¼ cups	dry split yellow peas, soaked 8 hours in cold water	300 mL
6 cups	chicken stock, heated	1.5 mL
1	bay leaf	1
½ tsp	dried basil	2 mL
1 tsp	chopped fresh parsley	5 mL
	salt and freshly ground pepper	
1 cup	cooked ham, julienned	250 mL
	few drops Worcestershire sauce	
2 tbsp	soft butter	30 mL

- Heat bacon fat in large saucepan over medium heat. Add onion and cook 3 minutes.
- Stir in celery and carrot; cover and cook 4 minutes, stirring once or twice.
- Stir in drained soaked peas. Add chicken stock and all seasonings including bay leaf. Add ham; partly cover and cook soup 45 minutes over medium heat. Stir several times during cooking.
- Add Worcestershire sauce and butter; mix well and serve hot.

Celeriac Rémoulade with Shrimp

4 servings

These tiny, tender cold-water shrimp are sold cooked and peeled and should not be heated. In Quebec, these shrimp are called "crevettes de Matane", named for a town on the Gaspé peninsula.

1	medium celeriac (celery root)	1
½ cup	mayonnaise	125 mL
2 tsp	Dijon mustard	10 mL
1 tbsp	chopped fresh parsley	15 mL
	salt and freshly ground pepper	
	juice of 1 lemon	
	few drops of Tabasco sauce	
1½ cups	cold-water shrimp	375 mL

- Peel celeriac and cut into a fine julienne. Place in a large bowl.
- Mix remaining ingredients, except shrimp, in another bowl. Season to taste and add to celeriac. Mix well.
- Add shrimp, stir and correct seasoning. Serve on lettuce leaves.

Cipaille or Cipâte

12 to 20 servings

A variety of game was traditionally used in this layered pie. Feel free to substitute other meats for the poultry called for in this version of the recipe, increasing cooking time as appropriate.

1	large chicken, 5 to 6 lbs (2.5 to 3 kg)	1
1	partridge or duck	1
1	pork fillet	1
1 cup	flour, seasoned with salt and pepper	250 mL
10	slices fatty salt pork	10
4	onions, chopped fine	4
½ cup	chopped fresh parsley	125 mL
1 tsp	dried savory	5 mL
¼ cup	chopped celery leaves	50 mL
1 tbsp	salt	15 mL
½ tsp	pepper	2 mL
¼ tsp	cinnamon	1 mL
	pastry dough for 2 double-crust pies	
2 cups	grated cooked potato	500 mL
1 cup	chicken consommé	250 mL

- Cut the chicken and partridge or duck into individual servings and then bone them. Grind the pork fillet in a meat grinder or food processor.
- Dredge the poultry in the flour. Melt the salt pork in a skillet, remove the meat and brown the poultry in the fat, keeping the two kinds of poultry separate. When cooked, place the browned poultry in separate bowls.
- Add the onions, parsley and savory to the remaining fat and sauté until softened. Remove to a bowl. In the same pan, brown the pork along with the celery leaves, salt, pepper and cinnamon.
- Preheat oven to 300°F (150°C).
- Roll out about a third of the pastry dough to a thickness of ½ in. (1 cm). Use it to line a baking dish or Dutch oven 4 to 5 in. (10 to 13 cm) deep. Spread the pork mixture over the bottom of the pastry. Sprinkle with a layer of potato. Top with a few slices of the browned salt pork and about a third of the onion mixture. Pour the consommé over everything.
- Cover with another layer of dough, rolled thin. Cover with the chicken. Sprinkle with more grated potato, salt pork and onion mixture.
- Cover with a third thin layer of dough. Top with the partridge or duck and the remaining potato, salt pork, and onion mixture.
- Top the dish with a thick layer of pastry dough (about ½ in. (1 cm) thick). Bake for 4 hours. Serve hot or cold.

Ham Steaks Glazed with Maple Syrup

4 servings

1 tbsp	maple syrup	15 mL
1 tbsp	melted butter	15 mL
	juice of ½ a lemon	
4	cooked ham steaks, ¾ in. (2 cm) thick	4
	freshly ground pepper	

- Preheat oven to 375ºF (190ºC).
- Mix maple syrup with butter and lemon juice. Place ham steaks on an ovenproof platter and brush mixture on both sides. Season with pepper.
- Change oven setting to broil. Set platter on oven rack in top third of the oven and broil 4 minutes on each side.
- Serve.

Tourtière

4 to 6 servings

These savoury pies are popular for Christmas or New Year's celebrations, and Quebec cooks often make several of them at a time.

½ lb	ground veal	250 g
½ lb	ground pork	250 g
1	medium onion	1
¼ cup	water	50 mL
¾ tsp	salt	4 mL
	pepper	
	pinch ground cloves	
	pinch savory	
	pastry for double-crust pie	
1	egg yolk	1

- Preheat the oven to 450ºF (230ºC).
- Mix together all the ingredients except for the pastry and egg yolk in a large pan. Cook over medium heat until the meat is cooked but not dry. Correct seasoning as needed.
- While the mixture cools slightly, line a pie plate with pastry. Pour the filling into the pastry shell and cover with the second layer of pastry. Crimp edges shut and make a few slashes in the top to allow steam to escape.
- With a fork, beat the egg yolk with a little water. Brush over the crust. Bake for about 20 to 25 minutes or until the crust is golden-brown.

Maple Syrup Baked Beans

6 to 8 servings

Quebec baked beans are traditionally cooked in a stoneware pot, though cast iron can be used instead. Long, slow cooking is the key.

4 cups	Navy beans	1 L
	water	
1 lb	salt pork	500 g
1 tbsp	dry mustard	15 mL
½ cup	maple syrup	125 mL
	salt and pepper	
2	cloves garlic	2
1	bay leaf	1
4	cloves	4
2	large onions	2

- Soak the beans overnight or for about 12 hours. Drain and place in a heavy cooking pot. Cover with cold water, bring to a boil and simmer for 1 hour. Drain.
- Preheat oven to 275°F (130°C).
- Slice the pork and place half of it in a stoneware pot or Dutch oven. Add the beans and then the rest of the salt pork.
- Sprinkle the dry mustard over the beans and then pour the maple syrup over top. Season with salt and pepper. Add enough water to cover the beans and add the garlic and bay leaf. Stick the cloves into the onions and bury them in the beans. Cover and bake for 8 hours.
- Check the water during cooking, adding more if necessary. Uncover for the last 30 minutes of cooking.

Pork Tenderloin with Bordelaise Sauce

4 servings

Quebec produces more pork than any other province.
Tenderloins are extremely lean, tender and flavourful cuts.

2	pork tenderloins	2
2 tbsp	olive oil	30 mL
3.5 oz	bacon, diced	100 g
2	shallots, peeled and chopped	2
½ lb	fresh mushrooms, cleaned and quartered	250 g
2	cloves garlic, peeled and sliced	2
¼ tsp	dried thyme	1 mL
1 tbsp	basil	15 mL
2 tbsp	all-purpose flour	30 mL
1 cup	dry red wine	250 mL
1 cup	beef stock, heated	250 mL
	salt and freshly ground pepper	

- Preheat oven to 350ºF (180ºC).
- Trim off any excess fat and the thin silver skin that covers the tenderloins.
- Heat oil in a large ovenproof sauté pan over medium heat. Add pork and sear on all sides. Remove pork from pan and set aside.
- Add bacon to hot pan and cook 3 minutes. Add shallots, mushrooms, garlic and seasonings. Stir and cook for 2 minutes.
- Sprinkle in flour and mix well. Incorporate wine and beef stock. Season well.
- Return pork to pan, cover and finish cooking in oven for 30 to 40 minutes or according to size. Serve.

Stuffed Leg of Lamb

4 servings

3 tbsp	butter	45 mL
4	shallots, chopped	4
2 tbsp	chopped fresh parsley	30 mL
1 tsp	rosemary	5 mL
2 tbsp	chopped basil	30 mL
½ lb	fresh mushrooms, chopped	50 g
	salt and freshly ground pepper	
8	cloves garlic, blanched and puréed	8
1½ cups	croutons	375 mL
1	egg, beaten	1
1	boned leg of lamb	1
1 tbsp	olive oil	15 mL
1	onion, diced	1
1	carrot, diced fine	1
2 tbsp	all-purpose flour	30 mL
1 cup	dry white wine	250 mL
2 cups	light beef stock	500 mL

- Heat butter in frying pan over medium heat. Add shallots and cook 2 minutes.
- Add parsley, rosemary, basil and mushrooms. Season and cook 4 minutes.
- Transfer mixture to food processor. Add garlic and croutons; blend 10 seconds. Add beaten egg and blend to incorporate. Season well and set aside.
- Preheat oven to 450°F (230°C).
- Lay boned lamb flat and spread stuffing over it evenly. Roll and tie up lamb.
- Place lamb in roasting pan and baste with oil. Sear for 10 minutes in oven.
- Reduce heat to 350°F (180°C) and season meat generously. Cook lamb for 12 minutes per pound (25 minutes per kilogram), including searing time. When meat is cooked, let stand on platter 10 minutes before carving.
- Place roasting pan on stove over high heat. Add vegetables and cook 4 minutes. Sprinkle flour over the vegetables and brown for 4 minutes over medium heat. Remove vegetables from pan and set aside.
- Add wine to roasting pan and cook 2 minutes over high heat. Stir in beef stock and return vegetables to pan. Mix well, season and cook 6 minutes.
- Strain sauce and serve with the sliced lamb.

Gaspé Provincial Park

Grilled Marinated Breast of Duck

4 servings

4	boneless duck breasts with skin	4
1¼ cups	orange juice or unsweetened apple juice	300 mL
1¼ cups	water	300 mL
2 tsp	crushed garlic	10 mL
2 tsp	dried oregano	10 mL
2 tsp	ground ginger	10 mL
2 tsp	honey	10 mL
¼ tsp	freshly ground pepper	1 mL

- Cut slits on the diagonal about halfway through the skin of each duck breast. Place duck in a shallow dish and set aside.
- In a bowl, combine remaining ingredients. Pour over duck breasts, cover and refrigerate for 6 hours.
- Cook duck on preheated barbecue grill for about 20 minutes, basting often with marinade and turning after 10 minutes.

Salmon Trout Fillets with Asparagus Purée

4 servings

Salmon trout is one of the varieties of freshwater fish that live in Quebec's many lakes and rivers.

1	bunch fresh asparagus, diced	1
2 tbsp	extra virgin olive oil	30 mL
1 tbsp	olive oil	15 mL
	salt and freshly ground pepper	
4	salmon trout fillets, about 6 oz (175 g) each, skinned	4
	juice of ½ a lemon	
	fresh chives	

- Cook asparagus in salted boiling water for 4 minutes. Drain, reserving ½ cup (125 mL) cooking liquid. Place asparagus and reserved liquid in blender and blend until smooth. Gradually add extra virgin olive oil, blending well after each addition. Strain purée through a sieve and set aside.
- Heat olive oil in a large frying pan over medium-high heat. Season fillets and cook 2 minutes on each side.
- Sprinkle fillets with lemon juice. Divide asparagus purée among 4 individual plates and place fillets on top. Garnish with fresh chives.

Potato and Peanut Butter Treats

These traditional candies are made from some unexpected ingredients.

⅔ cup	cold mashed potatoes	150 mL
7 cups	icing sugar	1.75 L
½ tsp	vanilla extract	2 mL
½ cup	peanut butter	125 mL

- In a large bowl, mix the mashed potatoes together with the sugar and the vanilla until thoroughly incorporated.
- Roll out the dough into a rectangle about ¼ in. (½ cm) thick. Spread the peanut butter over the rectangle evenly and roll up into a log. Refrigerate for 12 hours.
- Cut into slices about ½ in. (1 cm) thick and serve.

Maple Mousse

4 servings

3 tbsp	cornstarch	45 mL
2 tbsp	cold milk	30 mL
2 cups	skim milk	500 mL
½ cup	maple syrup	125 mL
4	egg whites	4
	pinch of salt	

- Dissolve the cornstarch in the cold milk; set aside. In a saucepan, heat the skim milk and maple syrup. As soon as the liquid comes to a boil, add the cornstarch mixture.
- Cook over low heat until the mixture thickens. Pour into a wide, shallow dish to allow it to cool quickly.
- Beat the egg whites with the salt until stiff peaks form. Fold in the cooled maple mixture. Divide among four dessert cups or ramekins and refrigerate. Serve cold.

Sugar Pie

6 to 8 servings

This old-style dessert is delicious served warm with a generous scoop of vanilla ice cream.

	pastry for single-crust pie	
1 cup	evaporated milk	250 mL
1½ cups	brown sugar	375 mL
1	egg	1
2 tbsp	flour	30 mL

- Preheat oven to 350ºF (180ºC).
- Line a pie plate with pastry. Set aside.
- Mix together the evaporated milk, brown sugar, egg and flour until the mixture is homogenous. Pour into the pie crust and bake for 35 minutes.

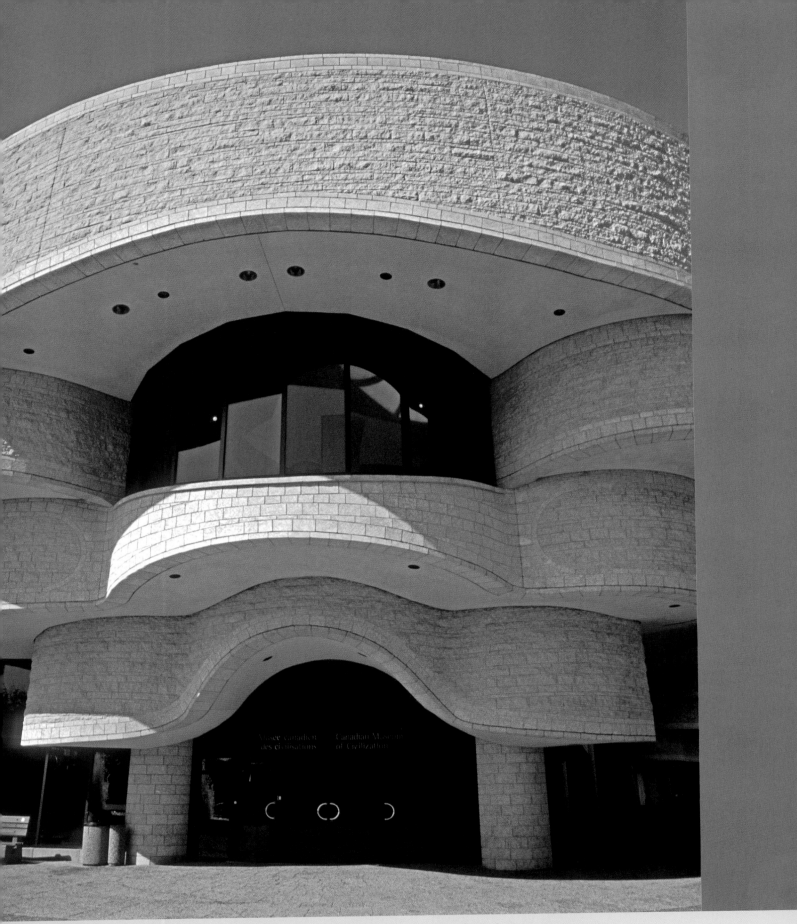

Canadian Museum of Civilization, Gatineau, Quebec

ONTARIO

The richest and most populous province in Canada.

Trilliums

ITINERARY Ontario

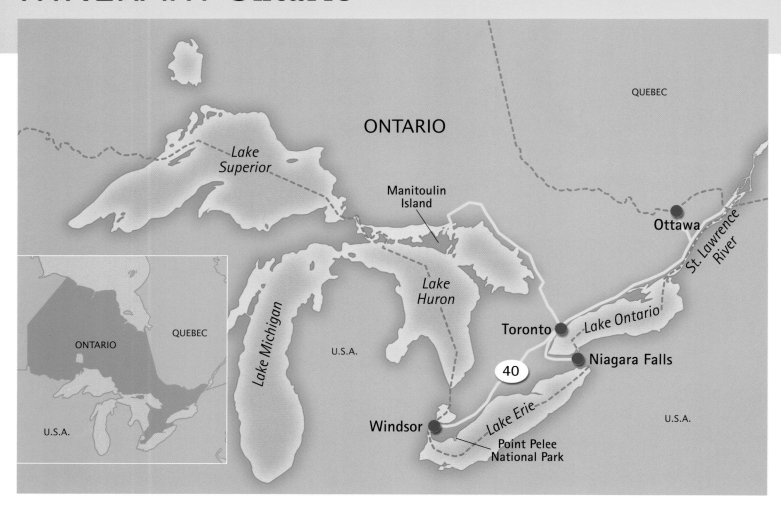

ONTARIO

Ontario was first settled around the Great Lakes, since it was easiest to explore the new territory by boat. Later, the construction of the railway towards the west allowed for the discovery of mineral deposits, which contributed to the province's growth, as did the forestry and agriculture industries.

Ontario has several geographical advantages. Thanks to the mild climate in the south, successful wineries have been established. Ontario wines have won many prizes and have become internationally renowned, with ice wine being its star product. The fertile land also produces a great variety of fruits and vegetables in abundance. In fact, Ontario agriculture is the most varied of the country.

The province's many lakes provide popular vacation spots. Visitors from around the world visit the cities of Toronto and Ottawa, and many make a detour to admire the world-famous Niagara Falls. The Niagara Peninsula has other attractions, including the wine route and numerous festivals.

Skating on the Rideau Canal, Ottawa

REGIONAL SPECIALTIES

Wine – Niagara wines have quickly earned an international reputation, in great part because of ice wine. This sweet dessert wine is made from grapes that have frozen, right on the vines, at temperatures of –10ºC (14ºF) for three days in a row. Freezing causes the sugars to be concentrated, giving this wine its characteristic taste. The technique was discovered in 1794, when German winemakers decided to make wine even though their grapes had frozen. Since then, winemakers in Germany and Austria make ice wine when winter temperatures get low enough. In fact, these two European nations are the only countries other than Canada whose climates allow this wine to be made using the traditional process.

Fruits and Vegetables – An abundance of all kinds of fruits and vegetables are grown in Ontario: apples, pears, peaches, plums, beets, cabbage, lettuce and carrots, among many others.

Turkey – Ontario is the country's top turkey producer.

What to See and Do

Manitoulin Island – This is the world's largest freshwater island. Located in the northern part of Lake Huron, it is an oasis of calm and an ideal spot for anyone who likes hiking, cycling, golf, nature or…relaxation.

Point Pelee National Park – Though small, with an area of only 20 km² (7.7 sq mi), this natural oasis is worth a visit. Located about 50 km southwest of Windsor, this park is the southernmost spot in Canada and enjoys a mild climate. In the spring and fall, it is a great spot to observe migratory birds, especially warblers, as well as monarch butterflies.

Pumpkinfest – Every October, Port Elgin, on the shores of Lake Huron, hosts this international quest for the biggest pumpkin. If you're lucky, you might get a glimpse of the pumpkin that will beat the record of 1000 lb (454 kg)!

Changing of the guard at Rideau Hall, Ottawa

Ottawa

Ottawa is Canada's capital, and numerous government departments and paragovernmental organizations are located there. It was selected as the capital in 1858 because it was located halfway between Toronto and Quebec City. The Parliament buildings are set on a hill overlooking the Ottawa river, and the site is particularly attractive in spring, during the annual Canadian Tulip Festival. During this event, many public spaces are transformed by the beautiful arrangements. And what is the origin of this festival? To thank Ottawa for providing a safe haven for the royal family during World War II and for the Canadian troops that helped liberate Holland, Princess Juliana of the Netherlands gave the city 100,000 tulips in 1945.

Canadian Tulip Festival, Ottawa

What to See and Do

Winterlude – For two weeks in February, this event is the perfect occasion to enjoy winter. You can admire the sculptures made from blocks of snow that are in the running for the annual contest or get some exercise skating or walking along the Rideau canal. The world's longest skating rink extends almost 8 km (5 mi) through downtown Ottawa. The frozen canal is the perfect place to eat a home-grown treat: beavertails. This flat fried pastry gets its name from its shape, and it is served with a choice of toppings.

Canada Day – The first of July is celebrated with gusto in the national capital.

The National Gallery of Canada – This museum's collection includes a significant concentration of Canadian art. The National Gallery also regularly welcomes world-class exhibitions from all over.

The Canadian Museum of Civilization – Just across the Ottawa river, you can learn about the fascinating history of the country, from prehistory to today.

Canadian Museum of Civilization, Gatineau, QC

Worth a Detour

The Thousand Islands – A cruise among these 1864 islands in the St. Lawrence will allow you to discover beautiful scenery, shipwrecks, mansions constructed thanks to profits from bootlegging and alcohol smuggling during prohibition, and much more.

Upper Canada Village Heritage Park – Come visit a reconstituted nineteenth century village with more than 40 historical houses and characters in period costumes. At this fascinating site, you'll learn about what life was like about 150 years ago.

Sandbanks Beaches Provincial Park – This site is known for its white sand dunes and its beautiful beaches on Lake Ontario. Close by is Lake on the Mountain Provincial Park—no one has ever discovered the lake's source, though there has been no lack of speculation over the centuries.

Parliament Buildings, Ottawa

Toronto harbour and CN Tower

Toronto

Ontario's capital, located on the shores of Lake Ontario, is Canada's metropolis and financial centre. It is also the country's most populous city, which attracts people from all over the world. In the twentieth century, especially after World War II, immigration to Toronto was very significant. Many new arrivals to Canada choose to settle in Toronto, giving the city a very cosmopolitan allure. There are restaurants where you can get an authentic taste of the foods of dozens of countries. The Toronto International Film Festival takes the city by storm every September.

What to See and Do

The Eaton Centre – This downtown shopping mall was inspired by a mall in Milan, Italy, and attracts many tourists every year.

CN Tower – At 553 m (1814 ft), the CN tower is the world's tallest building as well as being the defining element of the Toronto skyline. At the top, you can dine at the rotating restaurant while getting a 360° view of the city in 72 minutes. On lower levels are other cafés and observation decks.

SkyDome – This stadium, with its amazing retractable roof, is the venue for professional baseball and football games. It can hold up to 60,000 people for concerts and other cultural events in addition to sports showdowns. A hotel is integrated into the stadium.

The Toronto Islands – A ten-minute ferry ride from downtown Toronto will take you to the charming Toronto Islands. At the Toronto Islands Park, you can swim, picnic, cycle, in-line skate or go for a boat ride.

Worth a Detour

The Muskokas – North of Toronto, near Georgian Bay, you will discover the vacation spot of choice for many Torontonians. Charming cottages dot the shores of the many lakes, and there is no lack of opportunity to enjoy outdoor activities of all sorts.

Bruce Peninsula – In Tobermory, at the northernmost point of the Niagara escarpment, diving enthusiasts can explore more than 20 shipwrecks or any of the sea caves sculpted out of dolomitic limestone in the Five Fathom National Marine Park of Canada. The Bruce Peninsula National Park comprises several diverse and ancient habitats, home to 43 kinds of orchids as well as trees that are several hundred years old, including one that is over 850 years old.

Stratford Festival – Every year from April to October the town of Stratford, 150 km (93 mi) west of Toronto, plays host to many Shakespearean plays and other classic works.

The Niagara Peninsula Wine Route

The word Niagara instantly brings to mind the huge horseshoe-shaped falls plunging into the Niagara River. However, after taking in this wonder of the world, there are plenty of other things to visit in the Niagara Peninsula. This region benefits from a favourable microclimate and lots of fertile agricultural land, both of which allow for the cultivation of grapes destined for winemaking. You can tour the region's vineyards, and the route leading from one to another offers bucolic views with orchards and other crops scattered throughout, as well as numerous picturesque villages.

Worth a Detour

Niagara Falls – With an average height of 52 m, the falls are spectacular in all seasons. In January, during the dead of winter, the Festival of Lights illuminates the parks around the falls. Up until the 1950s, water erosion caused the falls to retreat by almost 1 m (3 ft) every year. Since then, hydroelectric power plants have been built upstream to regulate the flow and to slow down erosion. Nothing beats a boat ride on the *Maid of the Mist* to see the falls up close and feel the spray.

Niagara Grape and Wine Festival – This festival takes place every year in St. Catharines at harvest time, allowing you to discover and sample local products.

Shaw Festival – From April to December, Niagara-on-the-Lake puts on theatrical productions of the works of George Bernard Shaw and other playwrights.

Maid of the Mist

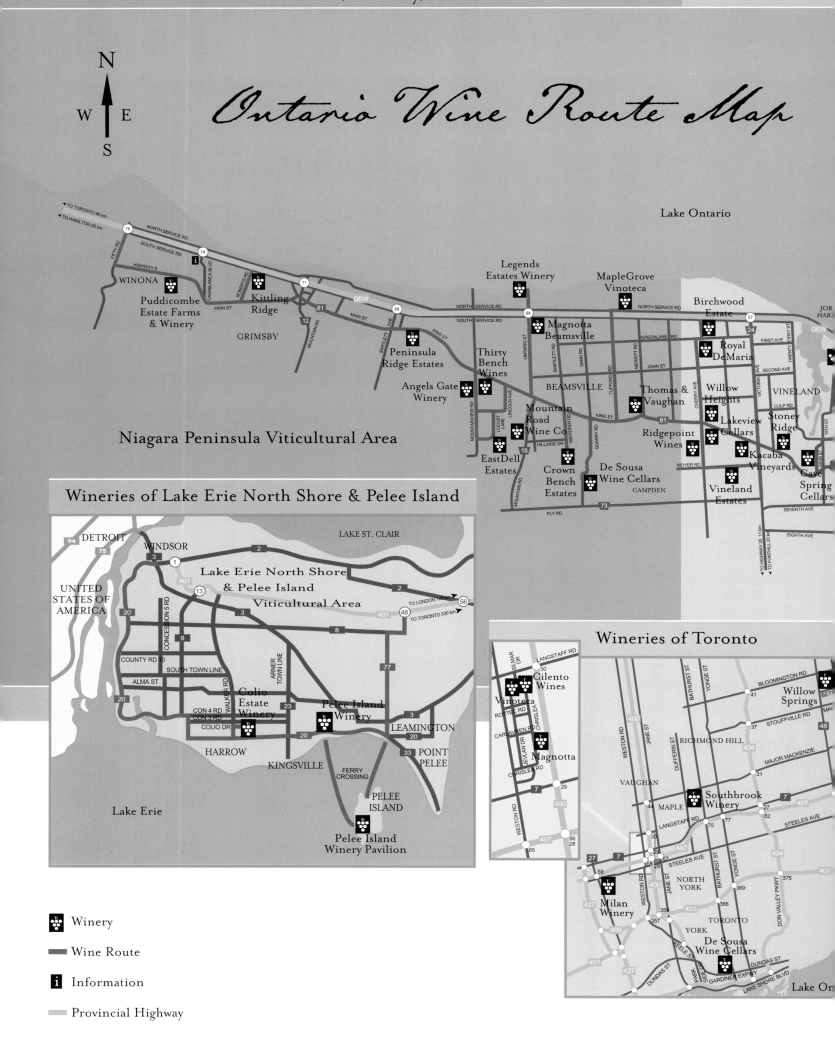

Ontario Wine Route Map

N
W   E
S

Lake Ontario

TO TORONTO 80 km
TO HAMILTON 25 km

NORTH SERVICE RD

SOUTH SERVICE RD

FIFTY RD

Highway 8

WINONA

CASABLANCA BLVD

ROBERTS RD

Puddicombe
Estate Farms
& Winery

Kittling
Ridge

MAIN ST

GRIMSBY

MOUNTAIN RD

QEW

MAIN ST

BARTLETT AVE

KING ST

Legends
Estates Winery

MapleGrove
Vinoteca

Birchwood
Estate

NORTH SERVICE RD

NORTH SERVICE RD

SOUTH SERVICE RD

Magnotta
Beamsville

Peninsula
Ridge Estates

Thirty
Bench
Wines

Angels Gate
Winery

ONTARIO ST

BARTLETT RD

SANN RD

GREENLANE RD

MERRITT RD

JOHN ST

Royal
DeMaria

Thomas &
Vaughan

BEAMSVILLE

CHERRY AVE

Willow
Heights

VINELAND

Niagara Peninsula Viticultural Area

MOUNTAINVIEW RD

LOCUST LANE

LINCOLN AVE

Mountain
Road
Wine Co

TUFFORD RD

KING ST

Ridgepoint
Wines

Lakeview
Cellars

Stoney
Ridge

CULP RD

NINTH ST

QUARRY RD

MOYER RD

Kacaba
Vineyards

Cave
Spring
Cellars

EastDell
Estates

HILLSIDE DR

MOUNTAIN RD

Crown
Bench
Estates

De Sousa
Wine Cellars

CAMPDEN

Vineland
Estates

SEVENTH AVE

FLY RD

EIGHTH AVE

TO HIGHWAY 20 11 km
TO FONTHILL 20 km

Wineries of Lake Erie North Shore & Pelee Island

LAKE ST. CLAIR

DETROIT

WINDSOR

UNITED
STATES OF
AMERICA

Lake Erie North Shore
& Pelee Island
Viticultural Area

TO LONDON 195 km
TO TORONTO 330 km

CONCESSION 5 RD

COUNTY RD 10

ALMA ST

ARNER TOWN LINE

WALKER RD

Colio
Estate
Winery

Pelee Island
Winery

LEAMINGTON

CON 4 RD
CON 5 RD
COLIO DR

HARROW

KINGSVILLE

POINT
PELEE

FERRY
CROSSING

PELEE
ISLAND

Lake Erie

Pelee Island
Winery Pavilion

Wineries of Toronto

SILMAR DR

LANGSTAFF RD

Cilento
Wines

Vinoteca

ROTTEC RD

CARLAUREN DR

LEVLAN DR

CHRISLEA

Magnotta

CHRISLEA RD

BLOOMINGTON RD

Willow
Springs

BATHURST ST

YONGE ST

STOUFFVILLE RD

RICHMOND HILL

WESTON RD

JANE ST

DUFFERIN ST

MAJOR MACKENZIE

VAUGHAN

MAPLE

Southbrook
Winery

STEELES AVE

WESTON RD

LANGSTAFF RD

NORTH
YORK

JANE ST

BATHURST ST

YONGE ST

DON VALLEY PKWY

Milan
Winery

TORONTO

YORK

De Sousa
Wine Cellars

PARK

DUNDAS ST

GARDINER EXPWY

LAKE SHORE BLVD

Lake On

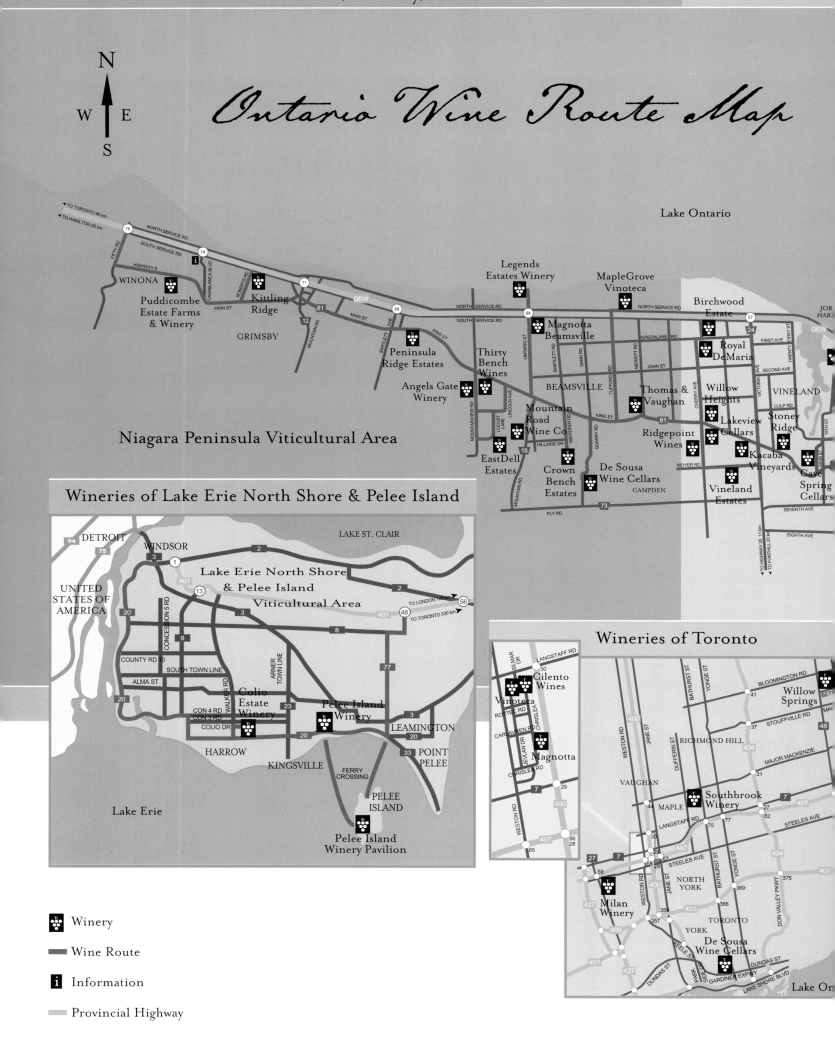

- Winery
- Wine Route
- Information
- Provincial Highway

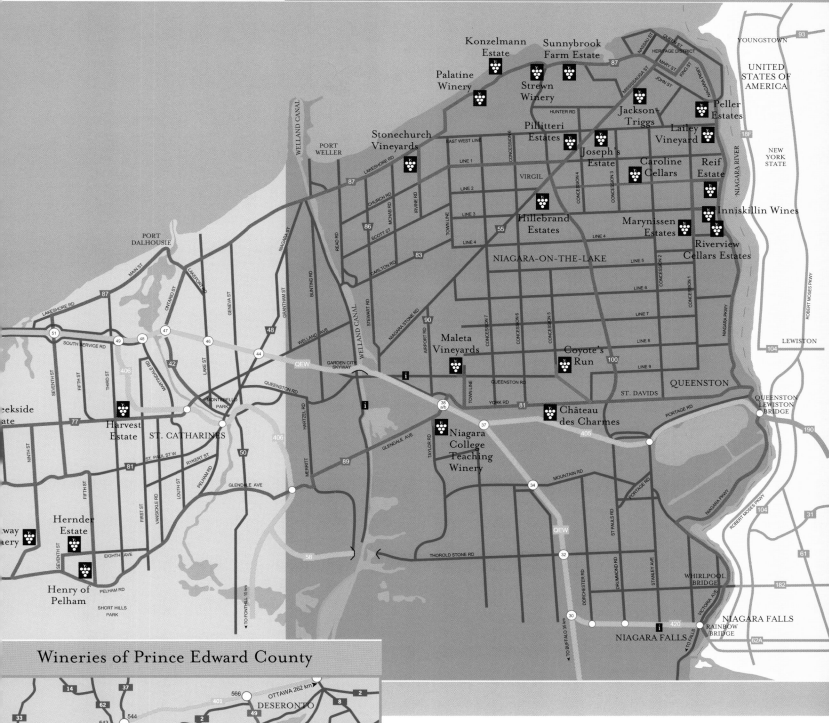

Wineries of Prince Edward County

Lake Ontario

Wine Route is a registered trademark and property of the Wine Council of Ontario. This map was reproduced with the permission of the Wine Council of Ontario. All rights reserved.

The Wine Council of Ontario urges all visitors not to drink and drive and suggests the use of a designated driver.

Estimated Driving Times:

Toronto–Niagara:	1 to 1-½ hours
Buffalo–Niagara:	½ hour
Toronto–Lake Erie North Shore:	4 hours
Detroit–Lake Erie North Shore:	½ hour
Toronto–Pelee Island:	4 hours, PLUS 1-½ hour ferry ride or 20 minutes on the hydrofoil
Toronto–Prince Edward County:	2-½ hours

The Canadian wine industry has developed strict quality standards. Since 1988, Ontario producers who respect these norms can display the VQA – Vintner's Quality Alliance – label.

Upper Canada Village

Cream of Squash Soup

4 to 6 servings

4 tbsp	butter	60 mL
1	sliced onion	1
6 cups	diced butternut or acorn squash (1 large butternut or 2 medium acorn)	1.5 L
	salt and pepper	
4 tbsp	flour	60 mL
5 cups	hot chicken stock	1.25 L
½ tsp	thyme	2 mL
1 tsp	basil	5 mL
½ tsp	celery seed	2 mL
¼ tsp	paprika	1 mL

- In a large pot, melt the butter over medium heat and cook the onion over low heat.
- Add the squash; season with salt and pepper. Cover and cook for 6 minutes over low heat.
- Sprinkle with flour and stir well. Cook for 1 minute.
- Add the remaining ingredients, bring to a boil and cook over low heat for 20 minutes.
- Purée and serve hot.

Cream of Carrot Soup

4 to 6 servings

3 tbsp	butter	45 mL
1	onion, chopped	1
6	carrots, peeled and chopped	6
1	stalk celery, finely chopped	1
½ tsp	basil	2 mL
1 tbsp	chopped parsley	15 mL
	salt and pepper	
3 tbsp	flour	45 mL
5 cups	hot chicken stock	1.25 L

- In a large pot, heat the butter over medium heat and cook the onion for 5 minutes over low heat.
- Add the carrots, celery, basil and parsley. Season with salt and pepper. Stir well and cook, partially covered, for 6 minutes over medium heat.
- Stir in the flour and the chicken stock. Correct the seasoning. Cover partially and bring to a boil. Reduce heat to low and cook for another 20 minutes.
- Purée and serve hot.

Chicken Melba

6 servings

6	boneless chicken breasts	6
1 cup	thinly sliced peaches	250 mL
6 oz	Camembert	180 g
2 tbsp	melted butter	30 mL
1 cup	raspberry coulis (see below)	250 mL
½ cup	heavy cream (35% MF)	125 mL

- Preheat the oven to 350°F (180°C).
- Flatten the chicken breasts. Arrange the peach slices and Camembert on the chicken breasts and roll.
- Place the rolled breasts on a greased cookie sheet, and brush with the butter. Cook for about 15 minutes.
- Pour the raspberry coulis into a saucepan. Add the cream and simmer for 5 minutes.
- Serve the chicken with the sauce.

Raspberry Coulis

(about 3 cups/750 mL)

2 lb	raspberries	1 kg
1 tbsp	cornstarch	15 mL
3 tbsp	Port	45 mL
¼ cup	sugar	50 mL

- In a food processor, purée the raspberries. Strain, discarding the pulp and seeds.
- In a saucepan, combine 3 cups (750 mL) of the raspberry juice, the cornstarch, sherry and sugar. Cook over low heat until the sauce thickens.

Green Beans in Sour Cream

4 servings

1 lb	green beans, washed and trimmed	500 g
	salt and pepper	
2 tbsp	butter	30 mL
3 tbsp	chopped onion	45 mL
1 tsp	vinegar	5 mL
1 tsp	sugar	5 mL
2 tbsp	flour	30 mL
1 cup	cooking water from beans	250 mL
½ cup	sour cream	125 mL
	paprika	

- Cook the beans, uncovered, in boiling salted water for 10 to 12 minutes. As soon as they are cooked, remove the saucepan from heat. Reserve 1 cup (250 mL) liquid. Place the beans in cold water. Drain well and set aside.
- In a saucepan, melt the butter over medium heat and cook the onion for 3 minutes over low heat.
- Add the vinegar and sugar and cook for 1 minute over medium heat.
- Add the flour, stir well and cook for 1 minute.
- Stir in the cooking liquid. Season with salt and pepper and cook for 7 minutes over low heat.
- Remove from heat. Add the sour cream, stir and sprinkle with paprika. Add the beans, stir gently and simmer for 3 minutes over low heat. Serve.

Tarragon Shallots and Mushrooms

4 servings

½ lb	peeled shallots	250 g
1 tbsp	butter	15 mL
8 oz	mushrooms, cleaned and halved	250 g
1 tbsp	chopped lemon zest	15 mL
1 tsp	tarragon	5 mL
¼ tsp	saffron	1 mL
	salt and pepper	

- Cook the shallots in salted boiling water for 10 minutes. Remove from heat and drain well.

- In a saucepan, melt the butter over medium heat. Add the shallots and the remaining ingredients. Cover and cook for 6 minutes.

Stuffed Roast Turkey

6 servings

Ontario is responsible for 40% of Canada's turkey production.

1	9-lb (4.5-kg) turkey, cleaned	1
1	recipe chestnut stuffing (see below)	1
½ lb	butter	250 g
	juice of 1 lemon	
	salt and pepper	

Stuffing

1 cup	long-grain rice	250 mL
2 cups	cold water	500 mL
1 tsp	salt	5 mL
6 tbsp	butter	90 mL
1	onion, finely chopped	1
1	large stalk celery, finely chopped	1
2 tbsp	chopped parsley	30 mL
½ tsp	sage	2 mL
½ tsp	thyme	2 mL
2	eggs, well beaten	2
4	slices bread, crusts removed, cubed and soaked in milk	4
2 cups	drained and chopped canned chestnuts	500 mL
	salt and black pepper	

Sauce

1	onion, cubed	1
1	stalk celery, cut into large chunks	1
1 tsp	basil	5 mL
½ tsp	celery seed	2 mL
½ tsp	thyme	2 mL
4 tbsp	flour	60 mL
2 cups	chicken stock	500 mL
	salt and pepper	

- To make the stuffing, spread the rice in a skillet and brown it over low heat.
- Place the water in a saucepan and add salt. Add the rice and bring to a boil. Cover and cook for 15 minutes over very low heat.
- In another saucepan, melt the butter over low heat and cook the onion, celery, parsley, sage and thyme for 4 minutes over low heat.
- Remove from heat; add the eggs, well-drained bread, chestnuts and rice. Season with salt and pepper and stir well. Allow to cool before stuffing the turkey.
- Preheat the oven to 400ºF (200ºC).
- Season the cavity of the turkey with salt and pepper before stuffing it. Gently separate the skin from the breast, taking care not to tear it. Slip slivers of butter between the skin and the meat. Truss and season the turkey well. Sprinkle with lemon juice.
- Place the turkey in a roasting pan. Roast in the oven for 30 minutes at 400ºF (200ºC). Lower the temperature to 325ºF (160ºC) and continue roasting for two and a half hours. It is important to baste the turkey every 15 minutes. If the turkey breast browns too quickly, cover it with aluminum foil. Once it is done, remove the turkey from the roasting pan.
- To make the sauce, place the roasting pan over high heat. Add the onion, celery, basil, celery seed and thyme. Cook for 7 minutes. Sprinkle with flour and cook for 4 minutes over medium heat. Add the chicken stock, season with salt and pepper; stir and cook for another 7 minutes.
- Strain the sauce and serve with the turkey, with the stuffing on the side.

Garlic Spinach

4 servings

4	bunches fresh spinach	4
1 tbsp	butter	15 mL
1 tbsp	mashed roasted garlic	15 mL
1	apple, peeled, cored and thinly sliced	1
2 tbsp	chopped green pepper	30 mL
	salt and pepper	
4 tbsp	slivered almonds	60 mL

- Remove the stems from the spinach. Wash well under cold water and drain. Steam or cook in boiling water. Drain well and set aside.
- In a skillet, melt the butter over medium heat and cook the garlic, apple, green pepper and almonds for 2 minutes.
- Add the spinach, season with salt and pepper and stir. Cover and cook for 3 minutes over low heat. Sprinkle with almonds and serve.

Georgian Bay Walleye Fillets

4 servings

Ontario is dotted with more than 400,000 lakes that are home to over 175 species of fish.

4	walleye fillets, 6 oz (170 g) each	4
	salt and pepper	
	juice of ½ a lime	
1 tbsp	butter	30 mL
½ cup	finely chopped shallots	125 mL
1 cup	diced mushrooms	250 mL
¼ cup	fish stock	50 mL
¼ cup	heavy cream (35% MF)	50 mL
2	cloves garlic, peeled and finely chopped	2
¼ cup	chopped fresh parsley	50 mL

- Season the fillets with salt and pepper and sprinkle with lime juice. Set aside.
- In a skillet, melt the butter over medium heat and cook the shallots and mushrooms until browned.
- Add the fish stock and cream. Reduce by one-third.
- Stir in the garlic and parsley and add the walleye fillets. Cover with parchment paper and simmer for 5 minutes. Turn the fillets over, cover again and cook for another 5 minutes.
- Arrange the fillets on dishes and top with the sauce.

Peach Upside-down Cake

6 to 8 servings

⅓ cup	butter	75 mL
⅓ cup	sugar	75 mL
1	large egg	1
1 tsp	vanilla	5 mL
1 cup	flour	250 mL
1 tbsp	baking powder	15 mL
½ cup	10% cream	125 mL
2	large egg whites, beaten into stiff peaks	2
¼ cup	brown sugar	50 mL
2 cups	peeled fresh peach quarters	500 mL
	sugar	

- Preheat the oven to 350ºF (180ºC). Grease a 9-inch (23-cm) cake pan.
- Place the butter, sugar, whole egg and vanilla in a large bowl. Mix for 2 minutes with an electric mixer until smooth.
- In another bowl, sift the flour and baking powder. Using a wooden spoon, stir half the flour into the first bowl. Stir in the cream and the remaining flour.
- Carefully fold in the beaten egg whites using a spatula. There should be no trace of egg white left.
- Sprinkle the brown sugar on the bottom of the greased cake pan. Arrange the peaches in the pan and pour the cake mixture over the peaches. Bake in the centre of the oven for 1 hour.
- As soon as the cake is done, remove it from the oven and let cool. Turn the cake out, upside down, onto a serving plate and sprinkle with a little sugar. Place in the oven 6 inches (15 cm) below the broiler. Broil for 3 minutes and serve.

Plum Tart

6 to 8 servings

	pastry for single crust pie	
¼ cup	apricot jam	50 mL
12 to 15	ripe yellow plums, halved and pitted	12 to 15
2 tbsp	sugar	30 mL
1	beaten egg	

- Preheat the oven to 400ºF (200ºC).
- On a lightly floured surface, roll out the pastry to a thickness of ⅛ inch (3 mm). Arrange in a fluted tart pan. Press down the dough lightly with the fingers, taking care not to tear it. Prick the pastry using a fork.
- In a small saucepan, melt the apricot jam. Remove from heat and let cool. Brush the pastry with a little jam. Arrange the plum halves on the crust, working inward from the edges. Top the plums with the remaining jam. Sprinkle with sugar.
- Brush the edges of the pastry with the beaten egg. Bake the oven for 35 to 40 minutes.

Apple Butter

1 litre/4 cups

4 cups	apple juice	1 L
4 cups	peeled, cored, diced apple	1 L
1 tbsp	lemon juice	15 mL
¾ cup	brown sugar	175 mL
1 tsp	allspice	5 mL
¼ tsp	ground ginger	1 mL

- In a large saucepan, reduce the apple juice to 2 cups (500 mL).
- Add the apples and bring to a boil. Reduce the heat and simmer for 30 minutes or until the apples are soft.
- Place the apple mixture in a food processor and purée until smooth. Add the remaining ingredients and mix well.
- Return to the saucepan and bring to a boil. Lower the heat and simmer for about 1 hour, until the mixture thickens.
- Pour into sterilized jars and seal.

Poached Pears with Chocolate Sauce

10 servings

4 cups	water	1 L
1½ cups	sugar	375 mL
2 tbsp	vanilla	30 mL
10	pears, peeled	10

Sauce

½ cup	sugar	125 mL
5 oz	semisweet chocolate	150 g
1	4½ oz (125 g) package cream cheese, at room temperature	1
1 tbsp	orange liqueur	15 mL
	vanilla ice cream	

- In a saucepan, heat the water, the sugar and the vanilla and bring to a low boil. Scoop out the cores of the pears with a melon baller and cut a thin slice from the bottom of each pear so that it sits upright. Place the pears in the saucepan and add more water to cover, if necessary. Cook for about 20 minutes, until the pears are soft, i.e. when a knife can be easily inserted. Drain, reserving 1 cup (250 mL) of the cooking liquid.
- To make the sauce, heat the reserved cooking liquid, sugar and chocolate in a saucepan over low heat. Once the chocolate has melted and the mixture is smooth and hot, add the cheese and liqueur. Whisk until well blended. Let cool. The mixture will thicken slightly as it cools.
- Place one pear and a scoop of ice cream on each plate. Top with the sauce.

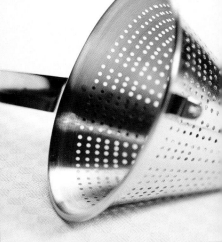

In the Muskokas

A pumpkin harvest

The PRAIRIES

*Manitoba, Saskatchewan and Alberta:
a land of plenty, and the world's breadbasket.*

Val Marie, Saskatchewan

MANITOBA

The territory that is now Manitoba formerly belonged to the Hudson's Bay Company. It was bought by the Canadian government to create the province in 1870. The railway's arrival in Winnipeg in 1881 brought with it great growth for the province. The railway also brought many immigrants from Eastern Europe to work the land. Agriculture—wheat-growing in particular—is the province's driving economic force. Manitoba also develops other resources, including forests and mines. Its many rivers have allowed it to produce so much hydro-electricity that 90% is exported to the United States.

Manitoba is where you will find Canada's longitudinal centre, the point that is equidistant from the west and east coasts. The province has a lot to offer: many kilometres of fine sand, a multitude of large lakes that provide excellent fishing and several historical sites of interest.

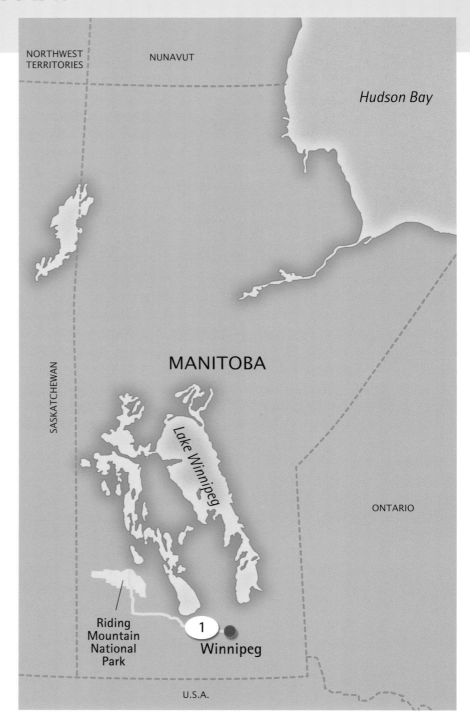

Provencher Bridge, Winnipeg

REGIONAL SPECIALTIES

Honey – About 75% of Canadian honey is produced in the Prairies, making Canada the fifth biggest honey-producing nation. Bees gather nectar from clover, canola and alfalfa, as well as playing an essential role in pollination. A third of Canadian production is exported to the United States and other countries.

Wheat – Wheat is the main crop of the province, though barley, oats and rye are also important crops, as are rapeseed and linseed. It's no accident that the Winnipeg grain exchange is among the largest in the world.

Pemmican – This is an old method for preserving food by drying it in the sun and wind. Natives often made pemmican from bison, moose or deer meat cut into thin slices and mixed with bison fat and berries. Trappers during the fur trade era adopted pemmican as a staple as it was rich in protein, easy to carry and available year-round. It is still made today for sled dogs during trips in the Far North.

What to See and Do

Winnipeg – This city is not only the province's capital, but it is also its main cultural centre, with several theatres, ballets and museums. Since Winnipeg is very cosmopolitan, you can choose from a wide selection of restaurants, which are often located in neighbourhoods favoured by ethnic communities. For example, *Saint-Boniface* is the French neighbourhood of Winnipeg.

Aurora borealis

The Forks National Historic Site – Located at the confluent of the Assiniboine and Red Rivers, this strategic site has always played a key role in transportation, commerce and the settlement of the region. Today, it is where Winnipeg holds various festivals and other events.

The Royal Canadian Mint – Canada's coins are made in Winnipeg, even though the Mint's headquarters is located in Ottawa. Take a guided tour to learn about all the steps involved in creating a coin.

Riding Mountain National Park – This mountain surrounded by vast fields is the best known and most visited park in Manitoba. About 200 km northwest of Winnipeg, it offers many walking and hiking paths, as well as lakes and herds of bison. The renowned conservationist Grey Owl worked here as a naturalist in 1931. The park was used as a POW camp for German prisoners of war from 1943 to 1945.

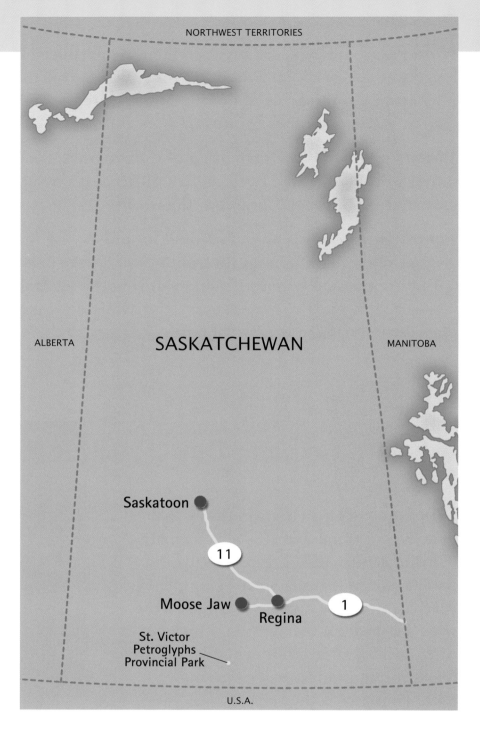

SASKATCHEWAN

When it entered the Canadian confederation in 1905, Saskatchewan attracted many Eastern European immigrants, in response to the government's western settlement policy. Settlers arrived and worked the fertile land—the population increased tenfold in just a few decades. Agriculture is ubiquitous in this province, which also has some of the world's biggest potash mines, making Canada the world's leading producer of this resource.

Saskatchewan's main feature is its mostly flat landscape, where sunsets are without equal. This province is for anyone who loves to see the horizon and who likes to take the time to live. And no, the province is not just one huge field: it includes over 100,000 lakes and rivers, to appeal to outdoors enthusiasts and fishers. In addition, Saskatchewan is a great place for recreational cycling. While riding on its calm roads, you'll cross nature parks, historical sites and charming villages where you can take a break and savour some local products.

REGIONAL SPECIALTIES

Saskatoons – This native shrub, from 0.5 m to 3 m (1.6 to 9 ft) high, produces delicious berries, which are dark purple when harvested in July and contain small seeds. They are prepared in many ways, often in jams, pies or to accompany game.

Wild Rice – The seed of an aquatic grass, wild rice was introduced to Saskatchewan in the 1920s. It grows in the shallow waters in the north of the province. Native North Americans have used canoes to harvest wild rice for centuries, but now specialized boats are used, which are equipped with beaters that knock the rice into a collecting tray. Harvesting is done in August and September.

Fruit Wine – Many fruits, such as raspberries, strawberries, chokecherries, crab apples and, of course, saskatoons, grow in abundance in Saskatchewan, and may be turned into delicious wines.

Castle Butte, Big Muddy Badlands

Castle Butte, Big Muddy Badlands

What to See and Do

Saskatoon – The most populous city in the province is also the heart of the agriculture industry. It is nicknamed the City of Bridges, thanks to the numerous bridges that cross the South Saskatchewan River, which runs through the city. The river is bordered by bike paths and parks.

Regina – Regina is the provincial capital. The legislative assembly building, erected in the twentieth century, is surrounded by beautiful gardens. The city has a certain English charm. The Wascana Centre, located in the city centre, is considered the largest urban park in North America and includes a lake and a bird sanctuary among other things. At the RCMP Museum, learn the history of the North West Mounted Police, which eventually became the Royal Canadian Mounted Police. You can also visit the RCMP Training Academy.

Moose Jaw – In downtown Moose Jaw, you'll find more than 35 murals that relate local history. Another peculiarity of this city is the network of tunnels that were built by Chinese immigrants who had come to build the railway at the end of the nineteenth century. In the 1920s, the tunnels were used to smuggle alcohol during Prohibition, and are said to have been visited by Al Capone.

St. Victor Petroglyphs Provincial Park – This mysterious site is home to more than 300 rock carvings of animals, humans, and animal and human prints. Scientists know little about these glyphs except that they are about 1000 years old and were made by a Native tribe that used to live on the Great Plains.

Saskatchewan Legislature, Regina

ALBERTA

Alberta was founded in 1905, the same year as Saskatchewan and in the same historical circumstances. Today, Alberta is nicknamed the Engery Province, thanks to its oil and natural gas deposits, which have made an important contribution to the economic growth of the province.

Ranching remains an important part of the Albertan economy and culture. You can even learn first-hand about farming and ranching life by touring farms or vacationing on a ranch. A rural holiday is also a great way to get a taste of local products and try outdoor activities such as horseback riding, hiking, fishing and nature study. Alberta is also the Rocky Mountains, with their spectacular landscapes that attract millions of tourists every year. A visit to one of the parks there will give you the chance to see all kinds of wildlife in its native habitat: mountain goats, elk, moose, bears and lynx, among others.

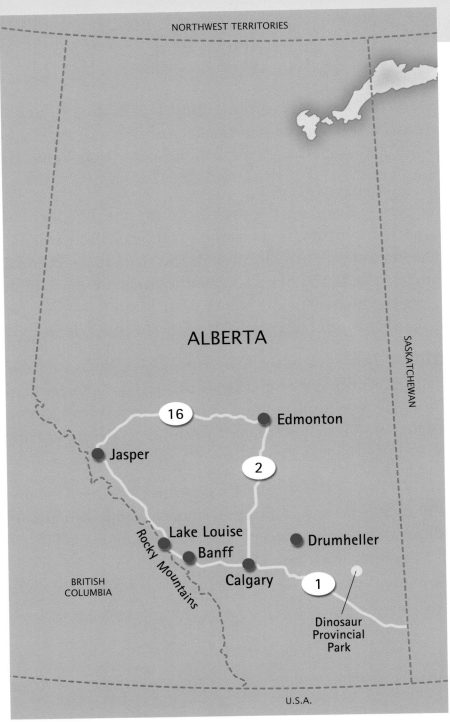

Fairmont Banff Springs Hotel

REGIONAL SPECIALTIES

Beef – With a world-class reputation, the province produces 40% of Canadian beef. In Alberta, Hereford and Angus cows are preferred, and their excellent meat satisfies the most distinguishing palates.

Taber corn – The city of Taber, in southern Alberta, is the self-proclaimed Corn Capital of Canada. Thanks to the quality of its soil and its climate, this region produces sweet and delicious corn. An annual festival is held at harvest time.

Wild mushrooms – The chanterelles and morels picked in the Rockies are a perfect accompaniment to delicious Alberta beef.

Goat cheese – Small, local producers are promoting this local product that is gaining in popularity.

Jasper Lake

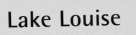
Lake Louise

What to See and Do

Calgary – This dynamic city is the venue for the renowned Stampede, a huge rodeo festival that takes place for two weeks every summer. Calgary also plays host to the Testicle Festival, where you can taste fried veal testicles, also called prairie oysters, which are a local delicacy. For a great view of the city and its surroundings, ride to the top of Calgary Tower.

Edmonton – The provincial capital is home to the world's largest shopping mall. Among other attractions, the West Edmonton Mall houses more than 800 stores, over 100 restaurants, hotels and an amusement park were you can bungee jump or take a submarine ride.

The Rocky Mountains – At the heart of the stunning mountains are many sites to visit: the charming towns of Banff and Lake Louise with their hot springs and the Château Lake Louise Hotel; Sunshine Village, the delight of skiers; numerous glaciers, including the Columbia Icefield; and Jasper National Park, where you can observe animals and vegetation and be allured by the pristine turquoise lakes. Several parks in the Rocky Mountains have been designated UNESCO World Heritage Sites.

Drumheller – In the Badlands lies Dinosaur Provincial Park (a UNESCO World Heritage Site), where dinosaur fossils abound. To learn all about these extinct creatures, visit the Royal Tyrell Museum, where you will find the world's largest reconstructed Tyrannosaurus Rex.

Borscht

10 servings

In the late nineteenth and early twentieth centuries, Western Canada was settled by numerous Eastern European immigrants. Their traditional dishes have been part of our culinary heritage ever since.

6	large beets	6
¼ cup	butter	50 mL
1 lb	diced beef	500 g
1	onion, chopped	1
¼	cabbage, sliced	¼
1	parsnip, diced	1
8 cups	chicken stock	2 L
1 tsp	sugar	5 mL
2 tsp	salt	10 mL
1 tsp	pepper	5 mL
1½ cups	sour cream	375 mL
1 tbsp	chopped fresh parsley	15 mL

- In a saucepan of boiling water, blanch the beets for 5 minutes. Drain, peel and dice.
- In a large pot, melt the butter and brown the beef cubes. Add the onion and beets and sauté for 5 minutes.
- Stir in the cabbage, parsnip and chicken stock. Simmer for 2 hours or until the beef is tender. Add the sugar, salt and pepper.
- When serving, add about 2 tbsp (30 mL) sour cream to each bowl. Sprinkle with parsley.

Rice Croquettes with Goat Cheese

6 servings

3 cups	white rice	750 mL
2 tbsp	heavy cream (35% MF)	30 mL
1	egg yolk	1
	salt and pepper	
3 oz	goat cheese, crumbled	90 g
1 oz	grated Parmesan	30 g

- Cook the rice according to the instructions on the package.
- In a bowl, beat the cream and egg yolk; season with salt and pepper.
- Add the rice and season again with salt and pepper. Stir in the goat cheese and Parmesan.
- Shape the mixture into small croquettes. Refrigerate for 30 minutes before frying in a skillet for a few minutes per side, or until the croquettes are golden.
- Serve with a basil tomato sauce or tartar sauce.

Bison Burgers

8 servings

2 lb	ground bison meat	1 kg
1 cup	breadcrumbs	250 mL
2	eggs	2
1 tbsp	Worcestershire sauce	15 mL
1 tsp	thyme	5 mL
½ tsp	cayenne pepper	2 mL

- In a large bowl, combine all the ingredients.
- Shape into patties.
- Barbecue for about 5 minutes per side, or to desired degree of doneness.

Roast Bison with Bourguignon Sauce

8 servings

3 tbsp	black peppercorns, crushed	45 mL
1	bison roast, 3 lb (1.5 kg)	1
3 tbsp	vegetable oil	45 mL
1 cup	beef stock	250 mL

Bourguignon Sauce

1 tbsp	butter	15 ml
1	large red onion, sliced	1
1 cup	mushrooms, sliced	250 ml
1 tbsp	flour	15 ml
½ cup	beef broth	125 ml
½ cup	red wine	125 mL
	salt and pepper	
	bouquet garni	

- Preheat the oven to 400ºF (200ºC).
- Season the roast with pepper and brush with vegetable oil.
- In a Dutch oven, sear the roast on all sides. Roast in the oven for 15 minutes per pound (500 g) if rare meat is desired.
- After the meat has been in the oven for 15 minutes, add 1 cup (250 mL) beef stock and a little salt. Baste frequently.
- To prepare the sauce, melt the butter in a saucepan and add the onion, mushrooms and flour. Stir in the beef stock and wine. Cook until the sauce thickens. Season with salt and pepper, add the bouquet garni and simmer for 10 minutes.
- Remove the bouquet garni and top the meat slices with the bourguignon sauce.

Drumheller, Alberta

Herbed Steaks

6 servings

½ cup	olive oil	125 mL
1 cup	red wine vinegar	250 mL
⅓ cup	brown sugar	75 mL
2	cloves garlic, crushed	2
1	onion, chopped	1
¼ tsp	cayenne	1 mL
¼ tsp	salt	1 mL
1 tsp	herbes de Provence	5 mL
6	strip-loin steaks, 8 oz (225 g) each	6

- Combine all the ingredients except the steaks in a saucepan and bring to a boil. Boil for 2 minutes. Remove from the heat and let cool.
- Place the steaks on a platter and drizzle with the marinade. Refrigerate for at least 6 hours. Cook the steaks in the oven, under the broiler or on the barbecue.

Rib-eye Roast

8 servings

¼ cup	flour	50 mL
2 tbsp	mustard powder	30 mL
1 tbsp	herbes de Provence	15 mL
½ tsp	salt	2 mL
4 lbs	rib-eye roast	2 kg
2 tbsp	Worcestershire sauce	30 mL
1	onion, chopped	1
2	carrots, chopped	2
1	leek, white part only, chopped	1
1	bay leaf	1
1 cup	red wine	250 mL
1 cup	water	250 mL

- Preheat the oven to 325°F (160°C).
- In a small bowl, combine the flour, mustard powder, herbes de Provence and salt. Rub the mixture onto the roast.
- Place the roast in a roasting pan. Sprinkle with Worcestershire sauce.
- Arrange the vegetables and bay leaf around the roast. Add the wine and water.
- Roast in the oven until the desired degree of doneness is reached, basting occasionally with the liquid.

Pike Fillets with Almonds

4 servings

4	fillets Nipiwan pike	4
½ cup	flour	125 mL
2 tbsp	butter	30 mL
1 tbsp	vegetable oil	15 mL
2 tbsp	toasted sliced almonds	30 mL
2 tbsp	capers	30 mL
	salt and pepper	
1 tsp	chopped fresh parsley	5 mL
	juice of ½ a lemon	

- Preheat the oven to 150°F (70°C).
- Dredge the fillets in flour.
- In a skillet, heat half the butter and all of the vegetable oil. Cook the fish over medium heat, 3 to 4 minutes per side.
- When done, place the fillets in the oven to keep warm.
- Heat the remaining butter in the skillet and cook the almonds and capers for 1 minute over medium heat. Season with salt and pepper.
- Add the parsley and lemon juice; correct the seasoning. Cook for another minute.
- Top the fillets with the sauce.

Mashed Potatoes with Corn and Cheddar

6 servings

4	red or white potatoes, unpeeled, quartered	4
⅓ cup	melted butter	75 mL
⅓ cup	sour cream	75 mL
1½ tsp	salt	7 mL
½ tsp	pepper	2 mL
¼ cup	milk	50 mL
8 oz	Cheddar, grated	250 g
8 oz	grilled corn kernels	250 g
⅓ cup	chopped parsley	75 mL

- In a pot of boiling water, cook the potatoes. Drain well.
- Mash the potatoes without removing skins. Add the butter, sour cream, salt, pepper and milk. The mixture should be slightly lumpy.
- Add the Cheddar, corn and parsley. Serve hot.

Buffalo Gap, Saskatchewan

Grilled Corn

4 to 12 servings

Corn grown in Taber, Alberta, is renowned for its exquisite taste.

4 to 12	cobs corn
	soft butter
	salt

- Choose nice, fresh cobs of corn. Do not remove the husks. Soak in cold water for 7 to 8 minutes.
- Preheat the grill to medium.
- Place the corn cobs on the hot grill. Cover and cook for 10 minutes, turning 3 times.
- Serve with butter and salt.

Three Kinds of Rice with Almonds

6 servings

Wild rice is actually a grain. The First Nations peoples were familiar with this plant, which grows in Saskatchewan's wetlands.

2 cups	hot, cooked long-grain rice	500 mL
2 cups	hot, cooked brown rice	500 mL
1 cup	hot, cooked wild rice	250 mL
2 tbsp	butter	30 mL
4 oz	oyster or button mushrooms, sliced	120 g
½ tsp	herbes de Provence	2 mL
1 tsp	salt	5 mL
¼ tsp	pepper	1 mL
1 cup	toasted sliced almonds	250 mL

- In a large bowl, combine the three kinds of rice. Keep warm.
- In a skillet, melt the butter and sauté the mushrooms until soft.
- Add the herbes de Provence; season with salt and pepper. Stir in the rice.
- Sprinkle with almonds and serve.

Wild Rice Salad

4 servings

Wild rice has a nutty taste and contains more protein than white or brown rice.

1 cup	wild rice	250 mL
8 cups	boiling water	2 L
1 tsp	salt	5 mL
1	orange	1
1½ cups	diced red, yellow and green pepper	375 mL
1	large apple, cored and diced	1
½ cup	chopped green onion	125 mL
½ cup	chopped parsley	125 mL
1 tbsp	lemon juice	15 mL

Dressing

1	egg	1
⅓ cup	unsweetened orange juice	75 mL
2 tbsp	wine vinegar	30 mL
1 tsp	hot mustard	5 mL
1 tsp	grated orange zest	5 mL
½ tsp	dried tarragon	2 mL
½ tsp	salt	2 mL
	pepper	
3 tbsp	water	45 mL
3 tbsp	vegetable oil	45 mL

- Rinse the wild rice under cold running water. Drain and place in boiling salted water. Cover, lower the heat and simmer for about 45 minutes. The rice should be tender but slightly chewy. Drain and let cool to room temperature.
- Place all the dressing ingredients except the oil in the food processor bowl. Run the food processor for a few seconds, adding the oil in a thin stream. Set aside.
- Slice the orange zest into thin strips for garnish. Peel the orange, removing all white pith. Set aside.
- Place the drained rice in a large bowl. Add the diced pepper, apple, green onion, parsley and lemon juice. Pour over the dressing and stir gently. Garnish with strips of orange zest and orange sections.
- Serve chilled or at room temperature.

Grain elevators, Saskatchewan

Perogies

4 to 6 dozen

Here's another recipe that comes to us from Eastern Europe.

Dough

4 cups	flour	1 L
½ tsp	salt	2 mL
1	egg, well beaten	1
1 cup	lukewarm water	250 mL

Filling

10	potatoes, boiled and mashed	10
2 cups	grated Cheddar, melted	500 mL
¼ cup	sour cream	50 mL
4	slices cooked bacon, crumbled	4
3 tbsp	fresh chives, chopped	45 mL
¼ cup	sliced mushrooms sautéed in butter	50 mL

Topping

¼ cup	butter	50 mL
2	large red onions, diced	2
2 cups	sour cream	500 mL
1 cup	cooked, crumbled bacon	250 mL

Dough
- In a deep bowl, combine the flour and salt. Add the egg and enough water to obtain a smooth dough.
- Knead the dough on a floured surface until smooth (do not overknead, which will make the dough tough).
- Place the dough in an oiled bowl and turn so that it is coated with oil. Cover the bowl and let the dough rest for 10 to 15 minutes.

Filling
- Combine all ingredients in a bowl.
- Roll out the dough on a lightly floured surface. Cut into 3-inch (7.5-cm) circles.
- Place a spoonful of the filling in the centre of each circle and fold over to form a half-moon, pinching the edges to seal.
- Drop a few perogies at a time into a large pot of boiling water. Stir gently with a wooden spoon to prevent sticking. Boil until the perogies puff up and float to the surface. Remove with a slotted spoon and drain well.

Topping
- In a skillet, melt the butter and sauté the onions over low heat until soft.
- Add the perogies and stir well. Serve with sour cream and crumbled bacon.

Cabbage Rolls

4 servings

Here's yet another dish that was brought to Canada by Eastern European immigrants.

1½ cups	salted boiling water	375 mL
¾ cup	long-grain brown rice	175 mL
1 tbsp	olive oil	15 mL
1 lb	lean ground pork	500 g
1	onion, chopped	1
1	carrot, grated	1
4	mushrooms, chopped	4
4	eggs, beaten	4
2 tbsp	grated Parmesan	30 mL
	Tabasco sauce	
	salt and pepper	
8	large cabbage leaves	8
¼ cup	chicken stock	50 mL
2 tbsp	tamari sauce	30 mL

- In a saucepan, bring the water to a boil. Add the rice and simmer for 35 minutes or until done.
- In a skillet, heat the olive oil over medium heat and sauté the pork, onion, carrot and mushrooms until cooked.
- Stir in the cooked rice and beaten eggs. Add the Parmesan; season with Tabasco, salt and pepper. Cover and set aside.
- Preheat oven to 300ºF (150ºC).
- In another saucepan of boiling water, blanch the cabbage leaves until they are soft enough to roll. Remove and place on a work surface, curved side down. Fill with the rice filling and roll, folding in the ends to keep the filling in.
- Place the cabbage rolls in a baking dish, folded side down. Combine the chicken stock and tamari sauce and pour over the rolls. Bake for about 30 minutes, or until tender.

Writing-on-Stone Park, Alberta

Crepe Batter

Prairie wheat is used to produce the flour that goes into numerous products.

1 cup	flour	250 mL
½ tsp	salt	2 mL
4	eggs	4
1 cup	sparkling mineral water	250 mL
1¼ cups	milk	300 mL
3 tbsp	warm melted butter	45 mL

- In a bowl, sift the flour and salt. Add the eggs and blend well. Whisk in the mineral water. Beat in the milk. Beat in the butter.
- Strain the batter through a fine sieve. Refrigerate for 1 hour before using.
- Note: If the batter is too thick, add a little water. Make sure the batter is smooth before using.
- Crepes are very versatile and may be served as a dessert with maple syrup, chocolate or caramel sauce or with your favourite fruit filling.

Strawberry Crepes

New strawberry cultivars withstand Prairie weather conditions, producing an abundance of this fruit for local markets.

½ lb	sliced fresh strawberries, or raspberries or saskatoons	250 g
8	crepes	8
1 cup	custard sauce (see below)	250 mL
	icing sugar	

- Preheat the oven to 400°F (200°C).
- Divide the berries among the crepes and top with custard sauce.
- Fold the crepes and arrange in an ovenproof dish. Sprinkle with icing sugar and bake in the oven for 6 minutes.

Custard Sauce

2 tbsp	flour	30 mL
¾ cup	sugar	175 mL
4	eggs	4
4 cups	hot milk	1 L
2 tsp	vanilla extract	10 mL

- In a bowl, sift the flour and sugar.
- In a stainless steel bowl, cream the eggs and sugar combined with the flour. Place the bowl over a saucepan half filled with boiling water.
- Gradually stir in the hot milk and add the vanilla. Cook until thickened. Do not allow to boil or the mixture will separate.

Saskatoon Pie

6 to 8 servings

To preserve their quality, saskatoons must be picked very early in the morning, before the heat of the day, and then frozen quickly.

	pastry for double-crust pie	
4 cups	saskatoons	1 L
¼ cup	water	50 mL
2 tbsp	lime juice	30 mL
½ cup	sugar	125 mL
¼ cup	maple sugar	50 mL
3 tbsp	flour	45 mL
	knobs of butter	

- Line a pie plate with half of the pastry. Preheat oven to 425ºF (210ºC).
- In a saucepan, simmer the saskatoons in water for 10 minutes. Add the lime juice.
- In a small bowl, combine the sugar, maple sugar and flour. Stir in the berries.
- Pour into a pie crust. Dot with knobs of butter. Cover with the top crust, seal and flute the edges.
- Bake for 15 minutes. Lower the oven temperature to 350ºF (175ºC) and continue baking for 35 to 45 minutes, until the crust is golden.

British Columbia

Columbia

A jewel nestled between the Rocky Mountains and the Pacific Ocean.

Tofino

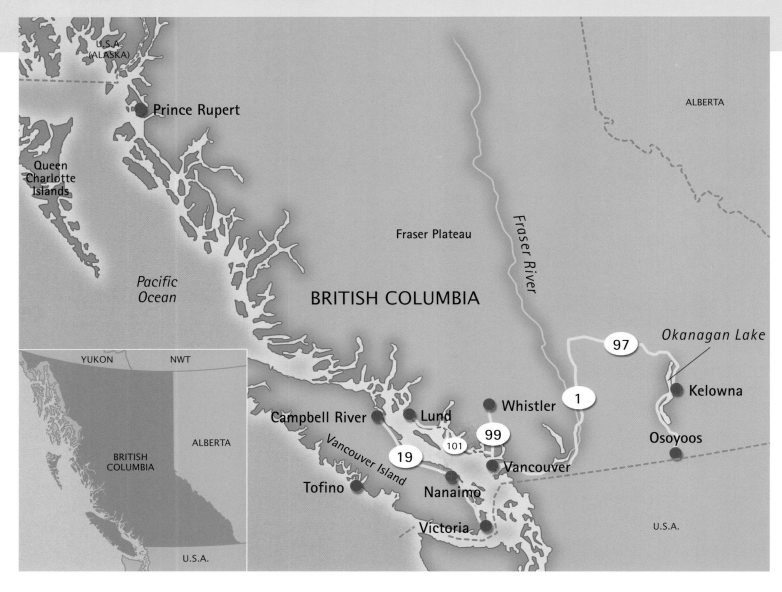

BRITISH COLUMBIA

In 1871, the Canadian government bought some of the land owned by the Hudson's Bay Company and thus founded the province of British Columbia. It promised to build a railway that would cross the Rockies, linking the Pacific with the eastern part of the country. The Canadian Pacific railway line was completed in 1885, thanks in large part to workers from China.

The terrain in British Columbia is so varied that the province comprises nine climatic zones. The majestic mountains are home to exceptional ski resorts. The different climates provide the province with all kinds of food: the rivers abound in salmon, a great variety of fruits and vegetables—as well as vineyards—flourish in the Okanagan valley and the ocean provides a wealth of shrimp, crabs and other top-notch seafood.

REGIONAL SPECIALTIES

Salmon – This fish is popular in many different forms: fresh, frozen, smoked, dried and canned. There is an abundance of different species of salmon in the rivers of British Columbia, and salmon farming is also successful in the province. Conservation measures have been instituted to ensure the health of BC's salmon stocks.

Dungeness Crab – Of the 35 species of crab that live in the waters off Canada's west coast, the Dungeness is the most prevalent. It is often sold alive.

Pacific Oyster – This oyster variety actually originated in Japan but has been cultivated in British Columbia since the 1920s.

Geoduck – This bivalve lives in burrows that it digs in the sand underwater. It is highly valued in Japan where it is eaten as sashimi, and it is harvested principally for export. The geoduck can grow to weigh 6 to 7 kg (13 to 15 lb) and can live 140 years.

Wine – British Columbia is the second wine-producing province in the country.

Butchart Gardens, Victoria

What to See and Do

Queen Charlotte Islands – Accessible by boat from Prince Rupert, this archipelago comprises 150 islands home to some subspecies of animals that are found nowhere else in the world. It has been called the Galápagos of Canada. At Old Masses, you can visit three ancient Haida villages. The Haida, a First Nations people residing primarily on the archipelago, are famous for their sculptures and beautiful totem poles.

Whale-watching – Cruises are available from several ports for those who want to see the beauty of the coast from the water and observe grey whales, humpback whales, orcas (killer whales) or sea lions.

Sunshine Coast, Highway 101 – This scenic drive runs along the coast, from Vancouver to Lund, a fishing village founded in 1889 by Swedish immigrants. All along the route you can admire islands, straits and charming villages. This area is the sunniest in the province, giving it its name.

Chesterman Beach, Tofino

Vancouver harbour

Vancouver

Vancouver is a large city on the Pacific coast where British, First Nations and Asian cultures come together. A modern city, Vancouver has close ties to Asia, partly because of its busy harbour. Vancouver achieves a perfect combination of urban life and nature, with an active cultural scene, numerous restaurants, cafés and shops as well as mountains for skiing and hiking, the sea for sailing and other water sports, beaches, and innumerable parks and gardens that provide green spaces for the city. Its location is ideal, nestled right between the sea and the mountains.

What to See and Do

Gastown – This historical neighbourhood was revitalized during the 1970s, and along its charming streets you will find shops, antique dealers, and cafés. The steam clock is one of Gastown's main attractions.

Grouse Mountain – Called the Skyride, the aerial tramway that will take you to the top of the mountain is the longest in North America. The 2 km (1.2 mi) ride provides a breathtaking view of the city, the ocean and the mountains.

Stanley Park – This oasis of green is a great place to rent a bike or inline skates and take the path that runs along the water. Or you can just rest on the beach.

Museum of Anthropology at the University of British Columbia – This institution is dedicated to relaying the life of the First Nations people of the Pacific Northwest. You can also appreciate several works by the Haida sculptor Bill Reid.

Local Food

Granville Island Public Market – The many stalls in this public market are laden with a multitude of fresh local products, fruits, vegetables, fish, seafood, meat, cheese and wine as well exotic foods.

Chinatown – Learn about Vancouver's Chinese community, with one of the biggest Chinatowns on the continent. The commercial streets are lined with restaurants and Asian grocery stores. Also in this neighbourhood is the Dr. Sun Yat-Sen Garden, whose layout is reminiscent of fifth century China, during the Ming dynasty. It harmoniously combines pavilions, covered passages, plants, water and rocks.

Stanley Park

Worth a Detour

Whistler Blackcomb – This ski resort, without a doubt one of the province's most celebrated, is only 120 km (75 mi) north of Vancouver. You can get there by taking the Sea to Sky Highway, which will take you from the coast to the clouds, as its name suggests.

The Fraser Valley – You can take in the beauty of the valley from below, by rafting down the Fraser river, or from above, on the Hell's Gate Airtram, where you'll get a bird's-eye view of the Fraser Canyon.

Swiftsure International Yacht Race

Royal British Columbia Museum and Empress Hotel

Victoria

The ferry ride from Vancouver will give you a glimpse of gorgeous coastal sights while taking you to the provincial capital of Victoria. This peaceful city, much smaller than Vancouver, has retained its British influence, as evidenced by its Victorian homes and English gardens. A walk around the harbour area will acquaint you with the local ambience. You can see the Parliament buildings and the Empress Hotel, both built during the nineteenth century. Victoria has one of the mildest climates in the country and rightfully deserves its moniker, the City of Gardens.

What to See and Do

Butchart Gardens – The 700 varieties of flowers in this garden are spectacular. In 1904, Jennie Butchart planted the first flowers in this depleted limestone quarry that had been run by her husband, Robert Butchart.

Royal British Columbia Museum – This museum is perfect for anyone with an interest in the history of the province.

Goldstream Provincial Park – Less than 20 km (12 mi) from downtown Victoria, from the end of October to December, you can watch salmon swim upstream among the splendid forest of Douglas firs and western red cedars.

Worth a Detour

Tofino – On the west coast of Vancouver Island, this lovely resort is renowned for its sunsets, its spectacular winter storms, its hot springs and its unspoiled natural splendour. The nearby Pacific Rim National Park Reserve has 20 km (12 mi) of beaches that make for some exceptional strolls.

Petroglyph Provincial Park – This Nanaimo site houses a collection of petroglyphs, ancient rock carvings. They are the work of First Nations people and, though experts cannot be absolutely certain, some petroglyphs are thought to be 3000 years old.

Campbell River – Located in the northeast of Vancouver Island, this town is considered the salmon capital of the world.

The Okanagan Valley

Nestled among the mountains, this dry valley has an exceptional climate that lends itself to the growing of fruits, especially grapes.

The British Columbia wine industry is still young: the first winemakers tried their hand at winemaking in the 1980s. Today, 18% of Canadian wine comes from British Columbia. Many producers have earned the right to use the VQA – Vintner's Quality Alliance – label since 1990.

What to See and Do

Okanagan Wine Country Tours – Nothing's better than a guided tour to discover some of the region's wineries, tour the facilities and taste some fine wine.

Kelowna – At the family-run Kelowna Land and Orchard Company Ltd., you can visit the orchards. You can also tour the small farm, have lunch at the picnic tables and buy some 100% pure juice at their shop. Also in Kelowna, you can watch jam being made from Okanagan fruit at the Jammery. The BC Orchard Industry and Wine Museum recounts the history of the fruit industry in the Okanagan valley.

Okanagan Lake – The biggest lake of the Okanagan is a great place for those who enjoy water sports.

Osoyoos – Near this town you'll find the Pocket Desert – the only desert in Canada. Though small, it is authentic, with surprising fauna and flora. Nearby is Spotted Lake, whose high concentration of minerals causes pale circles to form on the surface of the water in hot weather. Some native peoples considered this lake to have healing properties.

Chinese Chicken Soup

4 to 6 servings

One-third of Canada's Chinese immigrants make their home in Vancouver.

1 oz	dried Chinese mushrooms	30 g
10 cups	chicken stock	2.5 L
2	onions, chopped	2
2	carrots, sliced	2
1	leek, sliced	1
2 oz	Chinese noodles	60 g
2 cups	cubed cooked chicken	500 mL
12 oz	canned bamboo shoots, drained	350 g
	soy sauce	
	sambal oelek	

- Soak the mushrooms in a bowl of water for a few hours. Drain and slice.
- In a large pot, bring the chicken stock to a boil. Add the vegetables and lower the heat. Simmer for about 20 minutes.
- Stir in the noodles and the mushrooms. Return to a boil and cook for 10 minutes.
- Add the chicken, bamboo shoots and the soy sauce and sambal oelek to taste. Ladle into warmed bowls and serve hot.

Chinese Cabbage with Ginger

4 servings

1	Chinese cabbage (bok choy)	1
1 tbsp	olive oil	15 mL
1 tbsp	chopped, peeled fresh ginger	15 mL
1	clove garlic, peeled, crushed and chopped	1
	salt and pepper	
2	tomatoes, quartered	2
1 tbsp	teriyaki sauce	15 mL

- Separate the cabbage leaves and wash well. Remove the tips and use only the white part. Cut diagonally into large pieces.
- In a skillet, heat the olive oil over medium heat and cook the cabbage, covered, for 3 minutes.
- Add the ginger and garlic. Season with salt and pepper. Add the tomatoes and cook, uncovered, for 5 minutes over high heat.
- Add the teriyaki sauce and serve.

BC Oysters

4 servings

12	giant Pacific oysters	12
2 tbsp	butter	30 mL
1 tbsp	chopped dried shallots	15 mL
2 tbsp	tomato paste	30 mL
1 tsp	15% cream	5 mL
	salt and pepper	
	a few drops of Pernod	
1	egg yolk	1
2 tsp	chopped fresh parsley	10 mL
	a few drops of Worcestershire sauce	
	fresh chives	

- Rinse and shuck the oysters. Reserve the juice and one shell from each oyster.
- In a skillet, melt the butter and sauté the shallots until golden.
- Add the tomato paste and cream; season with salt and pepper. Cook to reduce the liquid.
- Add the Pernod.
- Divide half the mixture among the 12 shells, which have been thoroughly cleaned beforehand. Top each shell with an oyster.
- Heat the rest of the mixture and add the egg yolk, parsley and Worcestershire sauce. Do not let the sauce boil.
- Top the oysters with the sauce and broil in the oven. The oysters are ready when their edges begin to curl.
- Serve, garnished with chives.

Grilled Vegetables

4 to 6 servings

2 tbsp	olive oil	30 mL
2	cloves garlic, blanched, peeled and pureed	2
	juice of 1 lemon	
1 tbsp	Worcestershire sauce	15 mL
1	red pepper, cubed	1
1	green pepper, cubed	1
1	yellow pepper, cubed	1
1	zucchini, cut into ½-inch (1.25-cm) rounds	1
1	yellow summer squash, cut into ½-inch (1.25-cm) half-moons	1
4	shallots, quartered	4
24	snow peas	24
1	leaf Chinese cabbage, cut into large pieces	1
2	carrots, peeled, blanched and cut diagonally into ½-inch (1.25-cm) pieces	2
1	red onion, quartered	1
	salt and pepper	

- Preheat the barbecue to high.
- In a bowl, combine the olive oil, garlic, lemon juice and Worcestershire sauce.
- Place all the vegetables in a large bowl. Add the marinade; season with salt and pepper. Stir well.
- Arrange all the vegetables in a double-sided vegetable grill. Place the grill on the hot barbecue, cover partially and cook for 9 minutes per side. Serve.

Avocado, Grapefruit and Smoked Salmon Salad

4 servings

2	grapefruits	2
2	avocados, pitted, peeled and diced	2
½ lb	sliced smoked salmon	250 g
	salt and pepper	
1 tbsp	hot mustard	15 mL
¼ cup	olive oil	50 mL
	juice of 1½ lemons	
	romaine lettuce leaves	

- Remove a thin slice from the either end of the grapefruits. Using a sharp knife, peel the grapefruits, removing all the white pith, and separate into segments. Place in a bowl.
- Add the avocados and smoked salmon. Season generously with salt and pepper.
- In another bowl, combine the mustard, olive oil and lemon juice. Season with salt and pepper. Add more oil if the dressing is too strong.
- Pour the dressing over the salad, stir gently and serve on lettuce leaves.

Crab and Corn Chowder

6 servings

4 tbsp	butter	60 g
4	green onions, halved horizontally and sliced	4
2 cups	2% milk	500 mL
1 cup	chicken stock	250 mL
1 cup	fish stock	250 mL
2	medium potatoes, peeled and cubed	2
1 cup	fresh corn kernels	250 mL
2	sprigs thyme	2
	salt and pepper	
½ lb	cooked crabmeat	250 g
2 tsp	chopped fresh parsley	10 mL

- In a saucepan, heat the butter and cook the green onions until soft. Add the milk, chicken stock, fish stock, potatoes, corn and thyme. Season with salt and pepper. Simmer until the potatoes are done.
- Remove the thyme sprigs. Add the crabmeat and parsley. Serve.

Crab Cakes

6 servings

¼ cup	cream cheese	50 mL
1	red pepper, finely chopped	1
3 tbsp	chopped chives	45 mL
2 tbsp	chopped fresh parsley	30 mL
2 tsp	sambal oelek	10 mL
1	whole egg	1
1	egg yolk	1
½ cup	breadcrumbs	125 mL
1 lb	cooked crabmeat	500 g
	salt and pepper	
	breadcrumbs for coating	
	peanut oil	

- In a bowl, combine all ingredients expect the breadcrumbs for coating and peanut oil.
- Shape into small balls. Flatten and coat with breadcrumbs.
- In a skillet, fry the crab cakes in a little peanut oil over medium heat until both sides are browned.

Steamed Dungeness Crabs

4 servings

The Dungeness crab is the species most fished in the waters off British Columbia. It is named for a fishing port in Washington State.

4	Pacific Dungeness crabs, about 3 lbs (1.5 kg) each	4
1	leek, white part only, sliced	1
1	stalk celery, chopped	1
2 cups	water	500 mL
½ cup	dry white BC wine	125 mL
2 tbsp	chopped fresh parsley	30 mL
	salt and pepper	

- Make an incision between the belly and shell of each crab in order to remove the shell. Rinse under cold water to remove the organs.
- In a large saucepan, place the vegetables, water, wine and parsley. Season with salt and pepper. Add the crabs.
- Steam for 20 minutes. Serve piping hot.

Cedar-planked Salmon

2 servings

¼ cup	maple syrup	50 mL
¼ cup	salt	50 mL
¼ cup	olive oil	50 mL
	juice of ½ a lime	
2	salmon fillets	2
	cedar plank soaked in water	

- In a bowl, combine the maple syrup, salt, olive oil and lime juice. Add the salmon fillets and marinate for about 4 hours.
- Soak the cedar plank in lukewarm water for at least 1 hour.
- Preheat oven to 350ºF (175ºC).
- Place the salmon fillets on the cedar plank that has been brushed with the marinade. Bake for 20 minutes. Do not re-use the plank.

Salmon Cooked in Foil Pouches

4 servings

Pesto Butter

15	leaves basil, washed	15
3	cloves garlic, peeled	3
¼ tsp	cayenne	1 mL
4 oz	unsalted butter	120 g
	a few drops of lemon juice	
	salt and white pepper	

Salmon Steaks

4	salmon steaks	4
4 oz	pesto butter	120 g
8	slices tomato	8
4	slices red onion	4
4	lemon rounds	4
4	bay leaves	4
	salt, pepper and paprika	

- In a food processor, combine the basil and garlic. Add the remaining ingredients to the pesto butter and blend well.
- Preheat the grill to medium–hot.
- Place each salmon steak on a double sheet of aluminum foil. Place a spoonful of pesto butter on each steak, along with two slices of tomato, an onion slice, a lemon slice and a bay leaf. Season with salt, pepper and paprika. Seal to form pouches.
- Place the pouches on the hot grill. Cover and cook for 25 to 30 minutes. The pouches may also be baked in the oven at 325°F (160°C).

Old growth forest, Vancouver Island

Nanaimo Bars

12 to 16 squares

Bottom layer

½ cup	butter	125 mL
¼ cup	sugar	50 mL
¼ cup	cocoa	50 mL
1	egg, beaten	1
1½ cups	graham cracker crumbs	375 mL
1 cup	grated coconut	250 mL

- In a double boiler, melt the butter, sugar and cocoa. Fold in the egg. Stir until the mixture thickens and remove immediately from the heat. Fold in the remaining ingredients. Press into a square cake pan.

Middle layer

½ cup	butter	125 mL
3 tbsp	15% cream	45 mL
2 tbsp	vanilla pudding mix	30 mL
2 cups	icing sugar	500 mL

- In a bowl, cream together the butter, cream and pudding mix. Fold in the sugar. Beat until light and fluffy. Pour into the cake pan and spread evenly.

Top layer

1 cup	semi-sweet chocolate	250 mL
1 tbsp	butter	15 mL

- In a double boiler, melt the chocolate. Stir in the butter. Let cool. Pour into the cake pan and refrigerate for 2 hours. Cut into squares and serve.

The Okanagan Valley is home to many orchards that produce the fruits used in the recipes on this page.

Peach and Pear Salad

6 servings

6	peaches	6
6	pears	6
2 tbsp	lemon juice	30 mL
¾ cup	sugar	175 mL
2 cups	water	500 mL
½ tsp	ground cinnamon	2 mL
½ cup	red currant jam	125 mL

- Peel and slice the peaches. Core and slice the pears. Place the peaches and pears in a salad bowl. Sprinkle with the lemon juice. Refrigerate.
- In a saucepan, dissolve the sugar in the water over medium heat. Add the cinnamon and red currant jam. Bring to a boil and simmer over low heat until only one-third of the sauce remains. Cool.
- Pour the sauce over the fruit. Garnish with mint leaves, if desired.

Apples with Raspberry Coulis

4 servings

4	apples, peeled and quartered	4
3 tbsp	butter	45 mL
3 tbsp	sugar	45 mL
1 cup	raspberries	250 mL
¼ cup	hot water	50 mL
¼ cup	sugar	50 mL
¼ cup	chopped pistachios	50 mL
	vanilla ice cream	

- Preheat the oven to 350ºF (180ºC).
- In a skillet, cook the apples, butter and 3 tbsp (45 mL) sugar over medium heat, stirring constantly. Transfer to an ovenproof dish.
- Bake in the oven for 10 minutes. In the meantime, using an electric mixer or food processor, purée the raspberries, hot water and ¼ cup (60 mL) sugar. Strain the coulis through a sieve.
- To serve, divide the raspberry coulis among four dessert plates or bowls and top with the apples. Garnish with the chopped pistachios and serve with vanilla ice cream.

Western red cedar

Skeena river

The FAR NORTH

Yukon, the Northwest Territories and Nunavut are more than ice and snow…

Alexandra Falls, NWT

YUKON

Yukon was born of the gold rush, which began in the 1890s when a prospector found gold in the Klondike River. The Canadian government decided to create a separate territory to achieve better control of the new riches of the region.

Even today, mining remains the economic backbone of this region, though tourism is also important. Visiting Yukon can be a great adventure for Canadians, without even leaving the country—you can immerse yourself in the magic and mystery of the North.

This territory, where several First Nations peoples, Anglophones and Francophones rub shoulders, is a great place for those who love history, good food and open spaces.

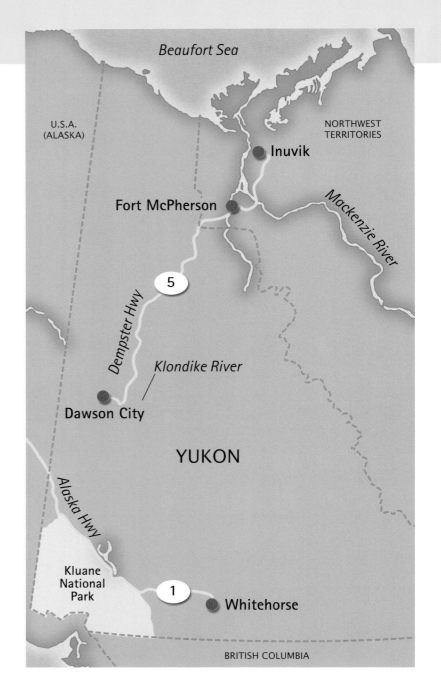

Moose along the Dempster Highway

REGIONAL SPECIALTIES

Bison – In Canada, bison is raised without the use of growth hormones or antibiotics. Bison meat is thus healthy and natural, in addition to being low in fat.

Caribou – This game meat is prepared in many ways in Yukon.

Salmon – The Yukon and Taku rivers abound with salmon.

Sourtoe Cocktail – In Dawson, you can try this mythical drink which contains a real human toe. This cocktail is said to have been invented in 1973 by Dick Stevenson, the captain of a river boat that tours the Yukon river. He found the toe in a house that he bought and ended up inventing this drink. If you try a sourtoe cocktail, at the Downtown Hotel's saloon, you can add your name to those of the other 15,000 people to have downed the drink (but not the toe!).

Microbrews – There are several microbrews that are available only in Yukon.

What to See and Do

Whitehorse – The capital city has a modern feel but is rich in history.

Kluane National Park – This park has been designated a UNESCO World Heritage Site. In addition to other mountains and wonders, Mount Logan, Canada's highest peak, lies within the park. There are also glaciers, bighorns, grizzly bears and moose. The Alaska Highway, which links Alaska and Whitehorse, makes it easy to reach the park from the capital.

Dawson – Dawson City is the place to go for the history of the gold rush. With its restored historical buildings, its saloons and its own particular feel, Dawson will plunge visitors into the fever of an era that lasted only a few years. The severe climate and the difficult operating conditions cut the craze short and few people really made their fortunes.

Dempster Highway – This road, 735 km (456 mi) long, from Dawson to Inuvik, NWT, can be rough. It will take you across the Arctic Circle and among the flora and the fauna that form part of the northern landscape.

Yukon Quest – The Yukon Quest is an international sled dog race that covers a distance of 1000 miles (1610 km). For two weeks every February, mushers and their 14 dogs race between Whitehorse and Fairbanks, Alaska, taking old mail routes and routes used during the gold rush. The itinerary takes the teams across mountains, and they must face strong winds and intense cold.

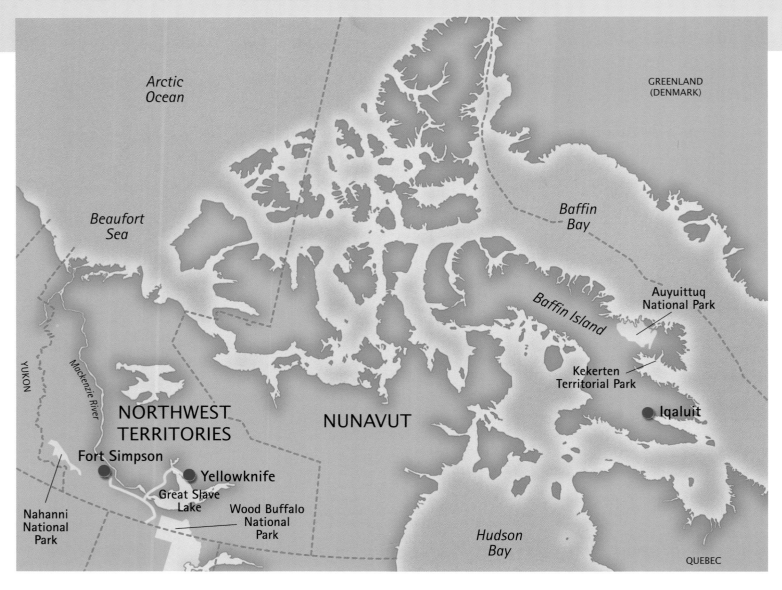

NORTHWEST TERRITORIES

This northern region has always been the realm of First Nations peoples who have been able to survive in the taiga and tundra. In 1870 the Canadian government bought great expanses of land from the Hudson's Bay Company and named them the Northwest Territories. In the twentieth century, southerners were attracted by the gold mines and military bases in the territories. The city of Yellowknife, on the shores of Great Slave Lake, developed thanks to mining in the area. With the discovery of diamonds in the 1990s, the territory's capital experienced its biggest boom yet. Today, only Russia and South Africa produce more diamonds than Canada.

A highlight of any trip to the Northwest Territories is the chance to be wonderstruck by the magnificent auroras borealis, or northern lights, which are visible for almost 300 nights a year in some parts of the territory. The Territories' numerous lakes also makes it a paradise for anyone who enjoys sport fishing.

Some of the Northwest Territory's diamond mines produce Polar Bear Diamonds. How can you identify a Polar Bear diamond? It has a tiny laser image of a polar bear on it!

REGIONAL SPECIALTIES

Bear – The Inuit have always hunted polar bears, whose meat is an excellent source of iron, protein and vitamin A. Their fur is used to make clothing that is perfectly adapted to the frigid temperatures of the North.

Muskox and Caribou – These game animals are widely consumed in the region.

A northern view

What to See and Do

Prince of Wales Northern Heritage Centre – Located in Yellowknife, this museum will help you learn about the history and culture of the native peoples of the Northwest Territories and of their way of life.

Waterfalls Route – The route between Fort Smith and Fort Simpson offers incomparable vistas: Alexandra and Louise falls in the Twin Falls Territorial Park, and Lady Evelyn and Sambaa Deh falls are not to be missed.

Cruises – You can take a cruise on the Yellowknife River, on the MacKenzie River or on Great Slave Lake to admire the fauna, the flora and the view.

Nahanni National Park – The natural beauty of this UNESCO World Heritage Site is breathtaking. Virginia Falls rush down the South Nahanni River from a height of 125 m (410 ft) in a spectacular show. The park is also home to canyons, vast cave systems and numerous hot springs.

Wood Buffalo National Park – The world's largest herd of free-roaming bison can be found in this National Park. It was created in 1922 to protect the boreal plains where the bison live. These plains have the distinctive characteristic of being salty, the only salt plains on the planet. The park, whose Visitor Reception Centre is in Fort Smith, has a network of hiking paths, and you can also paddle along the rivers in a canoe.

In 1999, the Canadian government divided the Northwest Territories into two, creating, in the eastern portion, Nunavut, where the majority of Canada's Inuit live. The creation of the new territory gave the Inuit their own government within the Canadian federation.

Iqaluit is the gateway to Nunavut in addition to being its capital. From there, visitors can chose from a variety of means to see the sights: canoeing, snowmobiling, dog sledding, hiking or cross-country skiing. Bear in mind, however, that there are no roads between cities, and the vast distances are best covered by plane. Hunting, fishing, petroleum development, mining and tourism are the main economic activities of the territory, which makes up 20% of Canada.

REGIONAL SPECIALTIES

Although the Inuit now eat a variety of imported foods, they continue to appreciate the traditional bounty of land and sea. And they are not alone!

Arctic Char – This fish, which lives in the cold waters around the Arctic Circle, has always been an important food staple for the Inuit. It wasn't exported to large North American cities until the 1940s. A member of the salmon family, Arctic char has a delicate taste, and its flesh can be red, orange-pink or white.

Black turbot from Baffin bay, *shrimp* and *scallops* are also local delicacies.

Muskox – Muskox can be found on many restaurant menus.

Caribou – Many caribou herds live in Nunavut. The lean meat makes a great stew.

What to See and Do

Iqaluit – This Baffin Island city, formerly called Frobisher Bay, was chosen to be the capital of Nunavut. Architects were inspired by the northern landscape and culture when designing the administrative buildings. In fact, the legislative building is reminiscent of an igloo and another government building is evocative of a snow drift.

Auyuittuq National Park – Nothing beats this park for viewing spectacular glaciers and fjords. The arctic landscape is stunning and you might get a look at whales, narwhals or even polar bears on ice floes.

Kekerten Territorial Park – At this park you'll find the remains of a Scottish whaling station established in the middle of the nineteenth century. An interpretive trail explains how whales were caught and how the whale meat and fat were used.

How did the Inuit get their vitamin C before fruits and vegetables arrived from the south? It came from muktuk, whale fat and skin that was dried for two days, then cooked and preserved in oil throughout the year.

Ice floes

Bannock

6 servings

Bannock is a bread made by First Nations peoples.

2 cups	corn flour	500 mL
1½ tsp	salt	7 mL
2 tbsp	baking powder	30 mL
¼ cup	lard	50 mL
⅔ cup	water	150 mL

- In a bowl, combine the corn flour, salt and baking powder.
- Add the lard all at once and mix well.
- Gradually add the water to obtain a smooth, slightly sticky dough.
- Shape into small ½-inch (1-cm) cakes.
- Fry in a skillet or bake in the oven at 300ºF (150ºC) for 2 to 3 minutes on a lightly oiled baking sheet.

Onondagas Muskox Loin

4 servings

The muskox is hunted in Nunavut.

2 lbs	muskox loin, bone out	1 kg
1	chili pepper, finely chopped	1
1 tbsp	horseradish	15 mL
3	cloves garlic, chopped	3
1 tsp	lime juice	5 mL
1 tsp	ground cumin	5 mL
2 tbsp	vegetable oil	30 mL
1 tbsp	coarse salt	15 mL
1 tsp	pepper	5 mL

- Cut the meat into 8 slices.
- In a bowl, combine the rest of the ingredients and coat the meat with the mixture.
- Marinate in the refrigerator for 2 hours.
- Grill for 2 minutes on the barbecue for well-done meat, or under the broiler to desired degree of doneness.

Nanuvik Bear Stew

4 servings

Here's a dish from the Northwest Territories.

1 lb	bear meat	500 g
¼ cup	vegetable oil	50 mL
	flour	
	salt and pepper	
½ tsp	rosemary	2 mL
½ tsp	thyme	2 mL
1 cup	chopped onion	250 mL
2	stalks celery, chopped	2
⅔ cup	red wine	150 mL
½ cup	halved cherry tomatoes	125 mL
⅔ cup	commercially prepared brown sauce	150 mL
4	servings cooked pasta	4
6	fresh mint sprigs	6

- Cut the bear meat into cubes. In a skillet, heat the vegetable oil and brown the meat on all sides. Sprinkle with flour.
- Remove the meat from the skillet and place in a bowl. Season with salt and pepper and add the rosemary and thyme.
- In the same skillet, cook the onions until golden. Add the celery.
- Deglaze the skillet with the red wine. Add the tomatoes, meat and brown sauce. Cook for about 2 hours, until the meat is tender.
- Correct the seasoning and serve with pasta. Garnish with fresh mint.

Tlingit Bison Stew

6 servings

This is a typical dish of the Tlingit, the First Nations people who live in Yukon and northern British Columbia.

Marinade

2 cups	red wine	500 mL
½ cup	vinegar	125 mL
	ground nutmeg	
½ tsp	allspice	2 mL
	salt and pepper	
3	cloves garlic, minced	3
4	carrots, sliced into rounds	4
2	stalks celery, cut into lengths	2
2 lbs	cubed bison meat	1 kg
12	pearl onions, peeled	12
7 oz	bacon	200 g
2 cups	beef stock	500 mL
1 tbsp	butter, softened	15 mL
1 tbsp	flour	15 mL

- In a bowl, combine all the marinade ingredients and marinate the meat for 4 hours, stirring two or three times.
- In a skillet, sauté the pearl onions and bacon. Set aside.
- Remove the meat from marinade, reserving the marinade. In a pot, sauté the bison until it is well browned.
- Add the marinade with the vegetables to the pot, along with the beef stock. Cook for 1½ hours, until the meat is three-quarters done.
- Remove the meat and strain the liquid.
- In a small bowl, combine the butter and flour to form a ball (beurre manié). Add it to the pot, stirring, to thicken the sauce.
- Add the meat, bacon and onions. Cook over low heat until the meat is tender, about 30 minutes.

Arctic Char in Dill Sauce

4 servings

This delicious fish is a staple of the Inuit diet.

2 lbs	Arctic char fillet	1 kg
	salt and pepper	
1 tsp	flour	5 mL
1 tsp	olive oil	5 mL
1 tsp	butter	5 mL
1	clove garlic, chopped	1
¼ cup	finely chopped shallot	50 mL

- Cut the fillet into 4 servings. Sprinkle with salt, pepper and flour.
- In a skillet, heat the olive oil and butter, and cook the fish for 5 minutes per side. Remove from the skillet and keep warm.
- In the same skillet, sauté the garlic, and shallot. Transfer to a plate and place the fish on top. Serve with dill sauce.

Dill Sauce

¼ cup	butter	50 mL
2	shallots, chopped	2
1	leek, sliced	1
1 cup	white wine	250 mL
1 cup	fish stock	250 mL
1 cup	heavy cream (35% MF)	250 mL
1 tbsp	butter	15 mL
1 tbsp	flour	15 mL
2	bunches dill, finely chopped	2

- In a skillet, melt the butter and cook the shallot and leek until translucent. Deglaze with the white wine and reduce by half.
- Add the fish stock and reduce by half again.
- Stir in the cream and simmer for 1 minute.
- In a small bowl, combine the butter and flour to make a ball (beurre manié). Stir it into the mixture to thicken the sauce.
- Add the dill just before pouring the sauce over the fish.

Polar bear and Northern lights

Inukshuk

Recipe Index

General Index

In this index, page numbers in italics refer to photos.

Photos

Photos reproduced in this book

Front cover
Waterton Lakes, Alberta
© John Sylvester

Back cover
Potato Farm, PEI
© John Sylvester

Gaspé Provincial Park
© John Sylvester

p. 6
Potato farm on PEI
© John Sylvester

p. 9
French River, PEI
© John Sylvester

p. 10–11
Magdalen Islands, QC
© John Sylvester

p. 12
Farm in Park Corner, PEI
© John Sylvester

p. 14
Windmills, Pincher Creek, Alberta
© John Sylvester

p. 15
Trinity Harbour
© John Sylvester

p. 17
Merritt's Harbour (detail)
© John Sylvester

p. 18–19
Gros Morne National Park
© John Sylvester

p. 21
A picturesque St. John's street
© John Sylvester

p. 22–23
Merritt's Harbour
© John Sylvester

p. 26
Newfoundland coast
© John Sylvester

p. 30
Deep Bay, Fogo Island, NF
© John Sylvester

p. 31
Peggy's Cove, NS
© John Sylvester

p. 33
Cabot Trail, Cape Breton
© John Sylvester

p. 34
Citadel Hill, Halifax
© John Sylvester

p. 34–35
Kejimkujik National Park, NS
© John Sylvester

p. 36
Cavendish Beach, PEI
© John Sylvester

p. 38–39
Hay bales, Park Corner, PEI
© John Sylvester

p. 40
Acadian village
© John Sylvester

p. 41
Sunset on Bay of Fundy
© John Sylvester

p. 42–43
Bay of Fundy
© John Sylvester

p. 50–51
Hopewell Rocks, NB
© John Sylvester

p. 53
Woodstock, NB
© John Sylvester

p. 57
Magdalen Islands
© John Sylvester